Introduction to ANSI C for Engineers and Scientists

Delores M. Etter

Department of Electrical and Computer Engineering
University of Colorado, Boulder

An Alan R. Apt Book

13 00

Prentice Hall, Upper Saddle River, NJ 07458

Library of Congress Cataloging–in–Publication Data

Etter, D. M.

    Introduction to ANSI C for engineers and scientists / Delores M. Etter.
        p.   cm.
    "An Alan R. Apt book."
    Includes index.
    ISBN (invalid) 0-13-241281-7 (paper)
    1. C (Computer program language)   I. Title.

QA76.73.C15E85   1995
620' .00285'5133--dc20

94-42851
CIP

Publisher: Alan Apt
Editor-in-Chief: Marcia Horton
Project Manager: Mona Pompili
Copy Editor: Shirley Michaels
Design Director: Amy Rosen
Designers: Meryl Poweski, Mona Pompili, Delores M. Etter
Cover Designer: Anthony Gemmelaro
Manufacturing Buyer: Donna Sullivan
Editorial Assistant: Shirley McGuire
Cover Photo: Satellite image of Earth's biosphere showing the distribution of vegetation and phyto-plankton (the microscopic plants that drift with the ocean currents and that are the basis of the ocean's complex food chain).

In memory of my dearest Mother, Muerladene Janice Van Camp

© 1996 by Prentice-Hall, Inc.
Simon & Schuster / A Viacom Company
Upper Saddle River, New Jersey 07458

The author and publisher of this book have used their best efforts in preparing this book. These efforts include the development, research, and testing of the theories and programs to determine their effectiveness. The author and publisher shall not be liable in any event for incidental or consequential damages in connection with, or arising out of, the furnishing, performance, or use of these programs.

Printed in the United States of America

10 9 8 7 6 5 4 3 2 1

ISBN 0-13-061607-9

PRENTICE-HALL INTERNATIONAL (UK) LIMITED, *London*
PRENTICE-HALL OF AUSTRALIA PTY. LIMITED, *Sydney*
PRENTICE-HALL CANADA, INC., *Toronto*
PRENTICE-HALL HISPANOAMERICANA, S.A., *Mexico*
PRENTICE-HALL OF INDIA PRIVATE LIMITED, *New Delhi*
PRENTICE-HALL OF JAPAN, INC., *Tokyo*
SIMON & SCHUSTER ASIA PTE. LTD., *Singapore*
EDITORA PRENTICE-HALL DO BRASIL, LTDA., *Rio de Janeiro*

TRADEMARK INFORMATION

MATLAB is a registered trademark of The MathWorks, Inc.

Preface

Engineers use computers to solve a variety of problems ranging from the evaluation of a simple function to solving a system of nonlinear equations. C has become the language of choice of many engineers and scientists not only because it has powerful commands and data structures, but also because it can easily be used for system-level operations. Because C is the language that a new engineer is most likely to encounter in a job, it is a good choice for an introduction to computing for engineers. Therefore, this text was written to introduce engineering problem solving with the following objectives:

- to present a consistent **methodology for solving engineering problems,**
- to introduce the **fundamental capabilities of C,** the language of choice of many practicing engineers and scientists, and
- to illustrate the problem-solving process with C through a variety of **engineering examples and applications.**

To accomplish these objectives, Chapter 1 presents a five-step process that is used in solving engineering problems, and Chapters 2–6 introduce the fundamental capabilities of C for solving engineering problems.

PREREQUISITES

No prior experience with the computer is assumed. The mathematical prerequisites are **college algebra and trigonometry.** Of course, the initial material can be covered much faster if the student has used other computer languages or software tools.

INTRODUCTION TO C

Many schools are using their introductory engineering courses to acquaint students with a variety of computer tools and languages. As a result, this text was developed as a brief introduction to C. Chapters 1–3 are necessary to be able to write substantial C programs, and Chapters 4–6 introduce additional topics, such as programmer-defined functions, one-dimensional arrays, and character data. In a typical introductory course, this material can be covered in six weeks. For a semester or quarter course devoted entirely to engineering problem solving with C, we recommend the text *Engineering Problem Solving with ANSI C: Fundamental Concepts.* In addition to more extensive coverage of the features of C, this expanded text also contains additional topics, such as two-dimensional arrays, matrices, pointers, dynamic memory allocation, character strings, and discussions of commonly used numerical techniques.

PROBLEM-SOLVING METHODOLOGY

The **emphasis on engineering and scientific problem solving** is an important part of this text. Chapter 1 introduces a **five-step process for solving engineering problems** using the computer:

1.   State the problem clearly.
2.   Describe the input and output information.
3.   Work a simple example by hand.
4.   Develop an algorithm and convert it to a computer program.
5.   Test the solution with a variety of data.

To reinforce the development of problem-solving skills, each of these five steps is clearly identified each time that a complete engineering problem solution is developed. In addition, **top-down design** and **stepwise refinement** are presented with the use of **decomposition outlines, pseudocode,** and **flowcharts.**

ENGINEERING AND SCIENTIFIC APPLICATIONS

Throughout the text, emphasis is placed on incorporating real-world engineering and scientific examples and problems. This emphasis is centered around a theme of **grand challenges,** which include:

- prediction of weather, climate, and global change
- computerized speech understanding
- mapping of the human genome
- improvements in vehicle performance
- enhanced oil and gas recovery

Each chapter begins with a photograph and a discussion of some aspect of one of these grand challenges that provides a glimpse of some of the exciting and interesting areas in which engineers might work. The grand challenges are also referenced in many of the other examples and problems.

ANSI C

The statements presented and all programs developed use the C standards developed by the **American National Standards Institute.** By using ANSI C, students learn to write **portable** code that can be transferred from one computer platform to another.

SOFTWARE ENGINEERING CONCEPTS

Engineers and scientists are also expected to develop and implement **user-friendly** and **reusable** computer solutions. Learning software engineering techniques is therefore crucial to successfully developing these computer solutions. **Readability** and **documentation** are stressed in the development of programs. Additional topics that relate to software engineering issues are discussed throughout the text and include issues such as **software life cycle**, **portability**, **maintenance**, **modularity**, **abstraction**, **reusability**, and **structured programming.**

EXERCISES AND PROBLEMS

Learning any new skill requires practice at different levels of difficulty. **Practice! problems** are short-answer questions that relate to the section of material just presented. Most sections are immediately followed by a set of Practice! problems so that students can determine if they are ready to continue to the next section. Complete solutions to all the Practice! problems are included at the end of the text.

Each chapter ends with a set of **end-of-chapter problems.** These are new problems that relate to a variety of engineering applications; the level of difficulty ranges from very straightforward to longer assignments. Each problem requires that the student develop a complete C program or function. Engineering data sets are included for many of the problems to use in testing.

STUDENT AIDS

Margin notes are used to help the reader not only identify the important concepts, but also to locate specific topics easily. In addition, margin notes are used to identify programming style guidelines and debugging information. Style guidelines show students how to write C programs that incorporate good software discipline; debugging sections help students recognize common errors so that they can avoid them. The programming style notes are indicated with the margin note *Style*, and the debugging notes are indicated with a **bug icon**. Each Chapter Summary contains a summary of the style notes and debugging notes, plus a list of the **Key Terms** from the chapter and a **C Statement Summary** of the new statements to make the book easier to use as a reference. Appendix A presents the **ASCII character codes**. In addition, the last two pages of the book contain information commonly used by students, including the operator precedence table, common C functions, common numeric conversion specifiers, and a C statement summary.

MATLAB AND VISUALIZATION

The visualization of the information related to a problem and its solution is a critical component in understanding and developing the intuition necessary to be a creative engineer. Therefore, we have included a number of plots of data throughout the text to illustrate the relationships of the information needed to solve specific problems. All the plots were generated using MATLAB, a powerful environment for numerical computations, data analysis, and visualization. For further information on MATLAB, we recommend two texts (also written by Delores M. Etter). *Engineering Problem Solving with MATLAB* provides a complete presentation on MATLAB, and *Introduction to MATLAB for Engineers and Scientists* is a brief introduction to the capabilities of MATLAB.

INSTRUCTOR'S MANUAL

An **Instructor's Manual** is available that contains complete solutions to all the end-of-chapter problems. Also, transparency masters are included to assist in preparing lecture material.

ACKNOWLEDGMENTS

I appreciate the encouragement of a number of people relative to the development of this text and would like to especially recognize Bernard Goodwin (who was the first person to begin telling me that I should write a C text) and Alan Apt (who convinced me that the time was right). I also want to acknowledge the outstanding work of the publishing team at Prentice Hall, including Marcia Horton, Dan Kaveney, Gary June, Mona Pompili, Alice Dworkin, and Mike Sutton. This text has been significantly improved by the suggestions and comments of the reviewers of *Engineering Problem Solving For Engineers and Scientists: Fundamental Concepts.* These reviewers included Arnold Robbins (Georgia Institute of Technology), Avelino Gonzalez (University of Central Florida), Thomas Cargill (Private Consultant), Jonathan Haines (Ball Aerospace Corp.), Thomas Walker (Virginia Polytechnic Institute and State University), Christopher Skelly (Insight Resource Inc.), Betty Barr (The University of Houston), John Cordero (University of Southern California), A. R. Marundarajan (Cal Poly, Pomona), Lawrence Genalo (Iowa State University), Karen Davis (University of Cincinnati), Petros Gheresus (General Motors Institute), Leon Levine (UCLA), Harry Tyrer (University of Missouri-Columbia), Caleb Drake (University of Illinois at Chicago), John Miller (University of Michigan-Dearborn), Elden Heiden (New Mexico State University), Joe Hootman (University of North Dakota), and Nazeih Botros (Southern Illinois University).

I also want to recognize the important contributions of the students in my introductory C programming course who class-tested and carefully reviewed the various drafts of this manuscript and gave their feedback on the explanations, the examples, and the problems.

Delores M. Etter
Department of Electrical/Computer Engineering
University of Colorado, Boulder

Contents

Introduction to ANSI C for Engineers and Scientists

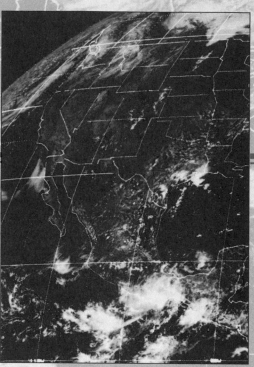

Courtesy of Texas Instruments Incorporated.

GRAND CHALLENGE:
Weather Prediction

Weather satellites provide a great deal of information to meteorologists who attempt to predict the weather. Large volumes of historical weather data can also be analyzed and used to test models for predicting weather. In general, we can do a reasonably good job of predicting the overall weather patterns; however, local weather phenomena, such as tornadoes, water spouts, and microbursts, are still very difficult to predict. Even predicting heavy rainfall or large hail from thunderstorms is often difficult. Although Doppler radar is useful in locating regions within storms that could contain tornadoes or microbursts, the radar detects the events as they occur and thus gives little time for issuing appropriate warnings to populated areas or aircraft. Accurate and timely prediction of weather and associated weather phenomena is still an elusive goal.

An Introduction to Engineering Problem Solving

OBJECTIVES

Although most of this text is focused on introducing you to the C language, we begin by presenting a group of grand challenges—problems yet to be solved that will require technological break-throughs in both engineering and science. One of the grand challenges includes the prediction of weather, which we used in the chapter opening discussion. Since most solutions to engineering problems use computers, we next describe computer systems with a discussion of both computer hardware and computer software. Solving engineering problems effectively with the computer also requires a design plan or procedure, and in this chapter we define a problem-solving methodology with five steps for describing a problem and then developing a solution.

1.1   Grand Challenges

Engineers solve real-world problems using scientific principles from disciplines that include computer science, mathematics, physics, and chemistry. It is this variety of subjects, and the challenge of real problems, that makes engineering so interesting and so rewarding. In this section we present a group of **grand challenges**—fundamental problems in science and engineering with broad potential impact. The grand challenges were identified by the Office of Science and Technology Policy in Washington, D.C., as part of a research and development strategy for high-performance computing. The following paragraphs briefly present some of these grand challenges and outline the types of benefits that will come with their solutions; additional discussions are presented at the beginning of the chapters. Just as the computer played an important part in the engineering achievements of the last thirty-five years, the computer will play an even greater role in solving problems related to these grand challenges.

Grand challenges

The **prediction of weather, climate, and global change** requires that we understand the coupled atmosphere and ocean biosphere system. This includes understanding CO_2 dynamics in the atmosphere and ocean, ozone depletion, and climatological changes due to the releases of chemicals or energy. This complex interaction also includes solar interactions. A major eruption from a solar storm near a "coronal hole" (a venting point for the solar wind) can eject vast amounts of hot gases from the sun's surface toward the earth's surface at speeds of over a million miles per hour. This ejection of hot gases bombards the earth with x-rays and can interfere with communication and cause power fluctuations in power lines. Learning to predict changes in weather, climate, and global change involves collecting large amounts of data for study and developing new mathematical models that can represent the interdependency of many variables.

Prediction of weather, climate, and global change

Computerized speech understanding could revolutionize our communication systems, but many problems are involved. Teaching a computer to understand words from a small vocabulary spoken by the same person is currently possible. However, to develop systems that are speaker-independent and that understand words from large vocabularies and from different languages is very difficult. Subtle changes in one's voice, such as those caused by a cold or stress, can affect the performance of speech recognition systems. Even assuming that the computer can recognize the words, it is not simple to determine their meaning. Many words are context-dependent and cannot be analyzed separately. Intonation, such as raising one's voice, can change a statement into a question. Although there are still many difficult problems left to address in automatic speech recognition and understanding, exciting applications are everywhere. Imagine a telephone system that determines the languages being spoken and translates the speech signals so that each person hears the conversation in his or her native language.

Computerized speech understanding

The goal of the **Human Genome Project** is to locate, identify, and determine the function of each of the 50,000 to 100,000 genes that are contained in human DNA (deoxyribonucleic acid), which is the genetic material found in cells. The

Human Genome Project

deciphering of the human genetic code will lead to many technical advances, including the ability to detect most, if not all, of the over 4,000 known human genetic diseases, such as sickle-cell anemia and cystic fibrosis. However, deciphering the code is complicated by the nature of genetic information. Each gene is a double-helix strand composed of base pairs (adenine bonded with thymine or cytosine bonded with guanine) arranged in a step-like manner with phosphate groups along the side. These base pairs can occur in any sequential order and represent the hereditary information in the gene. The number of base pairs in human DNA has been estimated to be around 3 billion. Because DNA directs the production of proteins for all metabolic needs, the proteins produced by a cell may provide a key to the sequence of base pairs in the DNA.

Substantial **improvements in vehicle performance** require more complex physical modeling in the areas of fluid dynamic behavior for three-dimensional flow fields and flow inside engine turbomachinery and ducts. Turbulence in fluid flows impacts the stability and control, thermal characteristics, and fuel performance of aerospace vehicles; modeling this flow is necessary for the analysis of new configurations. The analysis of the aeroelastic behavior of vehicles also affects new designs. The efficiency of combustion systems is also related because attaining significant improvements in combustion efficiency requires understanding the relationships between the flows of the various substances and the chemistry that causes the substances to react. Vehicle performance is also being addressed through the use of onboard computers and microprocessors. Transportation systems are currently being studied in which cars have computers with small video screens mounted on the dash. The driver enters the destination location, and the video screen shows the street names and path to go from the current location to the desired location. A communication network keeps the car's computer aware of any traffic jams so that it can automatically reroute the car if necessary. Other transportation research addresses totally automated driving, with computers and networks handling all the control and information interchange.

Enhanced oil and gas recovery will allow us to locate the estimated 300 billion barrels of oil reserves in the U.S. Current techniques for identifying structures likely to contain oil and gas use seismic techniques that can evaluate structures 20,000 feet below the surface. These techniques use a group of sensors (called a sensor array) that is located near the area to be tested. A ground shock signal is sent into the earth and is then reflected by the different geological layer boundaries and is then received by the sensors. Using sophisticated signal processing, the boundary layers can be mapped, and some estimate can be made as to the materials in the various layers, such as sandstone, shale, and water. The ground shock signals can be generated in several ways—a hole can be drilled, and an explosive charge can be exploded in the hole; a ground shock can be generated by an explosive charge on the surface; or a special truck that uses a hydraulic hammer can be used to pound the earth several times per second. Continued research is needed to improve the resolution of the information and to find methods of production and recovery that are economical and ecologically sound.

Improvements
in vehicle
performance

Enhanced oil
and gas recovery

These grand challenges are only a few of the many interesting problems waiting to be solved by engineers and scientists. The solutions to problems of this magnitude will be the result of organized approaches that combine ideas and technologies. The use of computers and engineering problem-solving techniques will be a key element in the solution process.

1.2   Computing Systems

Before we begin discussing the C language, a brief discussion on computing is useful, especially for those who have not had prior experience with computers. A **computer** is a machine that is designed to perform operations that are specified with a set of instructions called a **program**. Computer **hardware** refers to the computer equipment, such as the keyboard, the mouse, the terminal, the hard disk, and the printer. Computer **software** refers to the programs that describe the steps that we want the computer to perform.

Program

COMPUTER HARDWARE

All computers have a common internal organization, as shown in Figure 1.1. The **processor** is the part of the computer that controls all the other parts. It accepts input values (from a device such as a keyboard) and stores them in the **memory**. It also interprets the instructions in a computer program. If we want to add two values, the processor will retrieve the values from memory and send them to the **arithmetic logic unit**, or ALU. The ALU performs the addition, and the processor then stores the result in memory. The processing unit and the ALU use internal memory composed of read-only memory (ROM) and random access memory (RAM) in their processing. Most data are stored in external memory or secondary memory using hard disk drives or floppy disk drives that are attached to the

Arithmetic logic unit

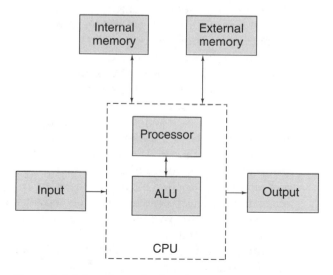

Figure 1.1 *Internal organization of a computer.*

processor. The processor and ALU together are called the **central processing unit**, or CPU. A **microprocessor** is a CPU contained in a single integrated circuit chip that contains millions of components in an area smaller than a postage stamp.

We usually instruct the computer to print the values that it has computed on the terminal screen or on paper using a printer. Dot matrix printers use a matrix (or grid) of pins to produce the shape of a character on paper, whereas a laser printer uses a light beam to transfer images to paper. The computer can also write information to diskettes, which store the information magnetically. A printed copy of information is called **hard copy,** and a magnetic copy of information is called an **electronic copy** or a soft copy.

Computers come in all sizes, shapes, and forms. (See photos on the next page.) Personal computers **(PCs)** are small, inexpensive computers that are commonly used in offices, homes, and laboratories. PCs are also referred to as microcomputers. Their design is built around a microprocessor, such as the Intel 486 microprocessor, which can process millions of instructions per second (mips). Minicomputers are more powerful than microcomputers; mainframes are even more powerful computers that are often used in businesses and research laboratories. A **workstation** is a minicomputer or mainframe computer that is small enough to fit on a desktop. **Supercomputers** are the fastest of all computers and can process billions of instructions per second. As a result of their speed, supercomputers are capable of solving very complex problems that cannot be feasibly solved on other computers. Mainframes and supercomputers require special facilities and a specialized staff to run and maintain the computer systems.

The type of computer needed to solve a particular problem depends on the problem requirements. If the computer is part of a home security system, a microprocessor is sufficient; if the computer is running a flight simulator, a mainframe is probably needed. Computer **networks** allow computers to communicate with each other so that they can share resources and information. For example, ethernet is a commonly used local area network (LAN).

(margin note: PCs)

(margin note: Networks)

COMPUTER SOFTWARE

Computer software contains the instructions or commands that we want the computer to perform. There are several important categories of software, including operating systems, software tools, and language compilers. Figure 1.2 illustrates the interaction between these categories of software and the computer hardware. We now discuss each of these software categories in more detail.

Operating Systems. Some software, such as the operating system, typically comes with the computer hardware when it is purchased. The **operating system** provides an interface between you (the user) and the hardware by providing a convenient and efficient environment in which you can select and execute the software on your system.

Operating systems also contain a group of programs called **utilities** that allow you to perform functions such as printing files, copying files from one diskette to another, and listing the files that you have saved on a diskette. Although these

Courtesy of Johnson Space Center.

Courtesy of The Image Works.

Courtesy of Apple Computer Inc.

Courtesy of The Image Works.

Courtesy of CRAY Research.

Courtesy of IBM.

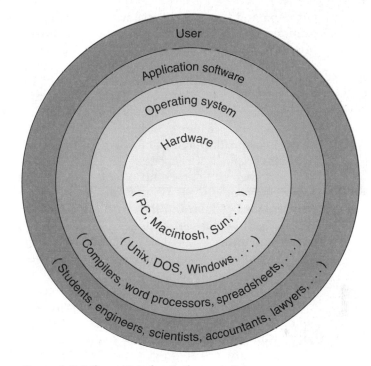

Figure 1.2 *Software interface to the computer.*

utilities are common to most operating systems, the commands themselves vary from computer to computer. For example, to list your files using DOS (a disk operating system used mainly with PCs), the command is **dir**; to list your files with UNIX (a powerful operating system frequently used with workstations), the command is **ls**. Some operating systems simplify the interface with the operating system. Examples of user-friendly systems are the Macintosh environment and the Windows environment.

Because C programs can be run on many different platforms or hardware systems and because a specific computer can use different operating systems, it is not feasible to discuss the wide variety of operating systems that you might use while taking this course. We assume that your professor will provide the specific operating system information that you need to use the computers available at your university; this information is also contained in the operating system manuals.

Software Tools. Programs that have been written to perform common operations are called **software tools**. For example, **word processors**, such as Microsoft Word and WordPerfect, are programs that have been written to help you enter and format text. Word processors allow you to move sentences and paragraphs and often have capabilities that allow you to enter mathematical equations and to check your spelling and grammar. Word processors are also used to enter computer programs and store them in files. Very sophisticated word processors allow you to produce well-designed pages that combine elaborate charts and graphics

Word processor

with text and headlines. These word processors use a technology called **desktop publishing**, which combines a very powerful word processor with a high-quality printer to produce professional-looking documents.

Spreadsheet

Spreadsheet programs are software tools that allow you to work easily with data that can be displayed in a grid of rows and columns. Spreadsheets were initially used for financial and accounting applications, but many science and engineering problems can be solved easily using spreadsheets. Most spreadsheet packages include plotting capabilities, so they can be especially useful in analyzing and displaying information. Lotus 1-2-3, Quattro Pro, and Excel are popular spreadsheet packages.

Database management

Another popular group of software tools are **database management** programs, such as dBASE IV and Paradox. These programs allow you to store a large amount of data, and then easily retrieve pieces of the data and format them into reports. Databases are used by large organizations such as banks, hospitals, hotels, and airlines. Scientific databases are also used to analyze large amounts of data. Meteorology data is an example of scientific data that require large databases for storage and analysis.

Computer-aided design

Computer-aided design (CAD) packages, such as AutoCAD, AutoSketch, and CADKEY, allow you to define objects and then manipulate them graphically. For example, you can define an object and then view it from different angles or observe a rotation of the object from one position to another.

Mathematical computation

There are also some very powerful **mathematical computation** tools, such as MATLAB, Mathematica, MATHCAD, and Maple. Not only do these tools have very powerful mathematical commands, but they also provide extensive capabilities for generating graphs. This combination of computational power and visualization power makes them particularly useful tools for engineers.

If an engineering problem can be solved using a software tool, it is usually more efficient to use the software tool than to write a program in a computer language to solve the problem. However, many problems cannot be solved using software tools, or a software tool may not be available on the computer system that must be used for solving the problem; thus, we also need to know how to write programs using computer languages. The distinction between a software tool and a computer language is becoming less clear as some of the more powerful tools, such as MATLAB and Mathematica, include their own language in addition to specialized operations.

Computer Languages. Computer languages can be described in terms of levels. **Low-level languages** or machine languages are the most primitive languages.

Machine language

Machine language is tied closely to the design of the computer hardware. Because computer designs are based on two-state technology (devices with two states, such as open or closed circuits, on or off switches, positive or negative charges), machine language is written using two symbols, which are usually represented using the digits 0 and 1. Therefore, machine language is also a **binary** language, and the instructions are written as sequences of 0's and 1's called binary strings. Because machine language is closely tied to the design of the computer hardware, the machine language for a Sun computer is different from the machine language for a Silicon Graphics computer.

An **assembly language** is also unique to a specific computer design, but its instructions are written in English-like statements instead of binary. Assembly languages usually do not have very many statements; thus, writing programs in assembly language can be tedious. In addition, to use an assembly language, you must also know information that relates to the specific computer hardware. Instrumentation that contains microprocessors often requires that the programs operate very fast; thus, the programs are called **real-time programs**. These real-time programs are usually written in assembly language to take advantage of the specific computer hardware in order to perform the steps faster.

High-level languages are computer languages that have English-like commands and instructions and include languages such as C, Fortran, Ada, Pascal, COBOL, and Basic. Writing programs in high-level languages is certainly easier than writing programs in machine language or in assembly language. However, a high-level language contains a large number of commands and an extensive set of **syntax** (or grammar) rules for using the commands. To illustrate the syntax and punctuation required by both software tools and high-level languages, we compute the area of a circle with a specified diameter in Table 1.1 using several different languages and tools. Notice both the similarities and the differences in this simple computation. Although we included C as a high-level language, many people like to describe C as a mid-level language because it allows access to low-level routines and is often used to define programs that are converted to assembly language.

Languages are also defined in terms of **generations**. The first generation of computer languages is machine language, the second generation of computer languages is assembly language, and the third generation of computer languages is high-level language. Fourth generation languages, also referred to as **4GLs**, have not been developed yet and are described only in terms of characteristics and programmer productivity. The fifth generation of languages is called natural language. To program in a fifth generation language, one would use the syntax of natural speech. Clearly, the implementation of a natural language would require the achievement of one of the grand challenges—computerized speech understanding.

Fortran (FORmula TRANslation) was developed in the mid-1950s for solving engineering and scientific problems. New standards updated the language over the years. The current standard, Fortran 90, contains strong numerical computation

---

TABLE 1.1 Comparison of Software Statements

Software	Example Statement
C	`area = 3.141593*(diameter/2)*(diameter/2);`
MATLAB	`area = pi*((diameter/2)^2);`
Fortran	`area = 3.141593*(diameter/2.0)**2`
Ada	`area := 3.141593*(diameter/2)**2;`
Pascal	`area := 3.141593*(diameter/2)*(diameter/2)`
Basic	`let a = 3.141593*(d/2)*(d/2)`
COBOL	`compute area = 3.141593*(diameter/2)*(diameter/2).`

capabilities, along with many of the new features and structures in languages such as C. **COBOL** (COmmon Business-Oriented Language) was developed in the late 1950s to solve business problems. **Basic** (Beginner's All-purpose Symbolic Instruction Code) was developed in the mid-1960s and was used as an educational tool. It is often included with the system software for a PC. **Pascal** was developed in the early 1970s and is widely used in computer science programs to introduce students to computing. **Ada** was developed at the initiative of the U.S. Department of Defense with the purpose of developing a high-level language appropriate to embedded computer systems, which are typically implemented using microprocessors. The final design of the language was accepted in 1979; it was named in honor of Ada Lovelace, who developed instructions for doing computations on an analytical machine in the early 1800s. **C** is a general-purpose language that evolved from two languages, BCPL and B, that were developed at Bell Laboratories in the late 1960s. In 1972, Dennis Ritchie developed and implemented the first C compiler on a DEC PDP-11 computer at Bell Laboratories. The language became very popular for system development because it was hardware independent. Because of its popularity in both industry and in academia, it became clear that a standard definition was needed. A committee of the American National Standards Institute (ANSI) was created in 1983 to provide a machine-independent and unambiguous definition of C. In 1989, the **ANSI C** standard was approved; that language is described in this text.

ANSI C

C has become the language of choice of many engineers and scientists because it has powerful commands and data structures and because it can be used easily for system-level operations. Because C is the language that a new engineer is most likely to encounter in a job, it is a good choice for an introduction to computing for engineers. However, it is more important to establish a good foundation in an introductory course in computing than it is to cover all the features of the language. Therefore, we have selected the most important features of C for solving engineering problems, and we have incorporated them in this text. Thus, we introduce you to the fundamental concepts of C, but we do not attempt to cover all elements of the language.

Executing a Computer Program. A program written in a high-level language such as C must be translated into machine language before the instructions can be executed by the computer. A special program called a **compiler** is used to perform this translation. Thus, in order to be able to write and execute C programs on a computer, the computer's software must include a C compiler. C compilers are available for the entire range of computer hardware, from supercomputers to personal computers. Most C compilers are based on the ANSI standards, but you should check the documentation of your compiler to see if it is an ANSI C compiler. If it is not an ANSI C compiler, there will be some differences between the C language that we discuss in this text and the C language accepted by the compiler.

Compiler

If any errors (often called **bugs**) are detected by the compiler during compilation, corresponding error messages are printed. We must correct our program statements and then perform the compilation step again. The errors identified during this stage are called **compile errors** or compile-time errors. For example,

Debugging

if we want to divide the value stored in a variable called **sum** by 3, the correct expression in C is **sum/3**; if we incorrectly write the expression using the backslash, as in **sum\3**, we will have a compiler error. The process of compiling, correcting statements (or **debugging**), and recompiling must often be repeated several times before the program compiles without compiler errors. When there are no compiler errors, the compiler generates a program in machine language that performs the steps specified by the original C program. The original C program is referred to as the **source program**, and the machine language version is called an **object program**. Thus, the source program and the object program specify the same steps, but the source program is specified in a high-level language, and the object program is specified in machine language.

Execution

Once the program has compiled correctly, additional steps are necessary to prepare the object program for **execution**. This preparation involves **linking** other machine language statements to the object program and then **loading** the program into memory. After this linking/loading, the program steps are executed by the computer. New errors, called execution errors, run-time errors, or **logic errors**, may be identified in this stage; they are also called program bugs. Execution errors often cause termination of a program. For example, the program statements may attempt to perform a division by zero, which generates an execution error. Some execution errors do not stop the program from executing, but they cause incorrect results to be computed. These types of errors can be caused by programmer errors in determining the correct steps in the solutions and by errors in the data processed by the program. When execution errors occur due to errors in the program statements, we must correct the errors in the source program and then begin again with the compilation step. Even when a program appears to execute properly, we must check the answers carefully to be sure that they are correct. The computer will perform the steps precisely as we specify, so if we specify the wrong steps, the computer will execute these wrong (but syntactically legal) steps and present us with an answer that is incorrect.

The processes of compilation, linking/loading, and execution are outlined in Figure 1.3. The process of converting an assembly language program to binary is performed by an **assembler** program. The corresponding processes are called assembly, linking/loading, and execution.

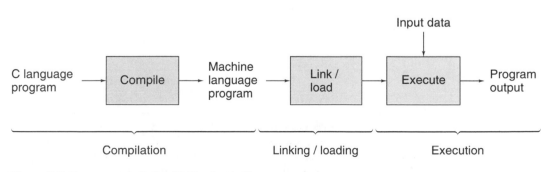

Figure 1.3 *Program compilation/linking/execution.*

A C compiler often has additional capabilities that provide a user-friendly environment for implementing and testing C programs. For example, some C environments contain text processors so that program files can be generated, compiled, and executed in the same software package, as opposed to using a separate word processor that requires the use of operating system commands to transfer back and forth between the word processor and the compiler. Many C programming environments include **debugger** programs, which are useful in identifying errors in a program. Debugger programs allow us to see values stored in variables at different points in a program and to step through the program line by line.

As we present new statements in C, we will also point out common errors associated with the statements or useful techniques for locating errors associated with the statements. The **debugging aids** will be identified with a bug icon in the margin, and they will also be summarized at the end of each chapter.

Software Life Cycle. In 1955, the cost of a typical computer solution was estimated to be 15% for software development and 85% for associated computer hardware. Over the years, the cost of the hardware has decreased dramatically, whereas the cost of the software has increased. In 1985, it was estimated that these numbers had essentially switched, with 85% of the cost for software and 15% for hardware. With the majority of the cost of a computer solution residing in software development, a great deal of attention has been given to understanding the development of a software solution.

The development of a software project generally follows definite steps or cycles, which are collectively called the **software life cycle**. These steps typically include project definition, the detailed specification, coding and modular testing, integrated testing, and maintenance. Data indicate that the corresponding percentages of effort involved can be estimated as shown in Table 1.2. From these estimates, it is clear that **software maintenance** is a significant part of the cost of a software system. This maintenance includes adding enhancements to the software, fixing errors identified as the software is used, and adapting the software to work with new hardware and software. The ease of providing maintenance is directly related to the original definition and specification of the solution, because these steps lay the foundation for the rest of the project. The problem-solving process that we present in the next section emphasizes the need to define and specify the solution carefully before beginning to code or test it.

One of the techniques that has been successful in reducing the cost of software development both in time and in cost is the development of **software prototypes**.

Software maintenance

Software prototypes

TABLE 1.2 Software Life Cycle Phases	
Life Cycle	Percent of Effort
Definition	3%
Specification	15%
Coding and Modular testing	14%
Integrated Testing	8%
Maintenance	60%

Instead of waiting until the software system is developed and then letting users work with it, a prototype of the system is developed early in the life cycle. This prototype does not have all the functions required of the final software, but it allows the user to use it early in the lifecycle and to make desired modifications to the specifications. Making changes early in the lifecycle is both cost-effective and time-effective.

As an engineer, it is very likely that you will need to modify or add additional capabilities to existing software. These modifications will be much simpler if the existing software is well-structured and readable and if the documentation that accompanies the software is up-to-date and clearly written. For these reasons, we stress developing good habits that make programs more readable and self-documenting. As new C statements are presented and new techniques are demonstrated, we include guidelines for writing well-structured and readable code. These **style guidelines** are indicated with margin notes and are also summarized at the end of each chapter.

1.3   An Engineering Problem-Solving Methodology

Problem solving is a key part of not only engineering courses, but also courses in computer science, mathematics, physics, and chemistry. Therefore, it is important to have a consistent approach to solving problems. It is also helpful if the approach is general enough to work for all these different areas, so that we do not have to learn one technique for mathematics problems, another for physics problems, and so on. The **problem-solving methodology** that we present works for engineering problems and can be tailored to solve problems in other areas as well. However, it does assume that we are using the computer to help solve the problem.

The process or methodology for problem solving that we will use throughout this text has **five steps**:

1.   State the problem clearly.
2.   Describe the input and output information.
3.   Work the problem by hand (or with a calculator) for a simple set of data.
4.   Develop a solution and convert it to a computer program.
5.   Test the solution with a variety of data.

We now discuss each of these steps using an example of computing the distance between two points in a plane.

1.   **PROBLEM STATEMENT**

The first step is to state the problem clearly. It is extremely important to give a clear, concise problem statement to avoid any misunderstandings. For this example, the problem statement is the following:

Compute the straight-line distance between two points in a plane.

2.   INPUT/OUTPUT DESCRIPTION

The second step is to describe carefully the information that is given to solve the problem and then identify the values to be computed. These items represent the input and the output for the problem and collectively can be called input/output or I/O. For many problems, a diagram that shows the input and output is useful. At this point the program is an "abstraction" because we are not defining the steps to determine the output; instead, we are only showing the information that is used to compute the output. The **I/O diagram** for this example follows.

I/O diagram

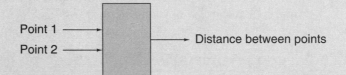

3.   HAND EXAMPLE

The third step is to work the problem by hand or with a calculator, using a simple set of data. This is a very important step and should not be skipped, even for simple problems. This is the step in which you work out the details of the problem solution. If you cannot take a simple set of numbers and compute the output (either by hand or with a calculator), then you are not ready to move on to the next step; you should reread the problem, and perhaps consult reference material. The solution by hand for this specific example follows:

Let the points p_1 and p_2 have the following coordinates:

$$p_1 = (1,5); \qquad p_2 = (4,7)$$

We want to compute the distance between the two points, which is the hypotenuse of a right triangle, as shown in Figure 1.4. Using the Pythagorean theorem, we can compute the distance with the following equation:

$$\begin{aligned}
\text{distance} &= \sqrt{(side_1)^2 + (side_2)^2} \\
&= \sqrt{(4-1)^2 + (7-5)^2} \\
&= \sqrt{13} \\
&= 3.61
\end{aligned}$$

4.   ALGORITHM DEVELOPMENT

Algorithm

Once you can work the problem for a simple set of data, you are then ready to develop an **algorithm**, a step-by-step outline of the problem solution. For simple

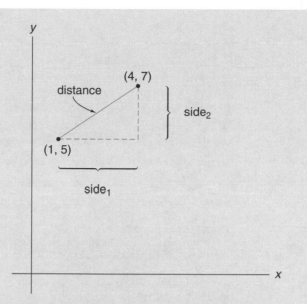

Figure 1.4 *Straight-line distance between two points.*

problems such as this one, the algorithm can be listed as operations that are per-formed one after another. This outline of steps decomposes the problem into simpler steps, as shown by the following outline of the steps required to com-pute and print the distance between two points.

Decomposition Outline
1. *Give values to the two points.*
2. *Compute the lengths of the two sides of the right triangle generated by the two points.*
3. *Compute the distance between the two points, which is equal to the length of the hypotenuse of the triangle.*
4. *Print the distance between the two points.*

This **decomposition outline** is then converted to C commands so that we can use the computer to perform the computations. From the following solution you can see that the commands are very similar to the steps used in the hand example. The details of these commands are explained in Chapter 2.

```
/*--------------------------------------------------------*/
/*   Program chapter1_1                                   */
/*                                                        */
/*   This program computes the                            */
/*   distance between two points.                         */
```

```c
#include <stdio.h>
#include <stdlib.h>
#include <math.h>

main()
{
   /*  Declare and initialize variables.  */
   double x1=1, y1=5, x2=4, y2=7,
          side_1, side_2, distance;

   /*  Compute sides of a right triangle.  */
   side_1 = x2 - x1;
   side_2 = y2 - y1;
   distance = sqrt(side_1*side_1 + side_2*side_2);

   /*  Print distance.  */
   printf("The distance between the two points is "
          "%5.2f \n",distance);

   /*  Exit program.  */
   return EXIT_SUCCESS;
}
/*--------------------------------------------------------*/
```

5.   TESTING

The final step in our problem-solving process is testing the solution. We should first test the solution with the data from the hand example because we have already computed the solution. When the C statements in this solution are executed, the computer displays the following output:

```
The distance between the points is  3.61
```

This output matches the value that we calculated by hand. If the C solution does not match the hand solution, we should review both solutions to find the error. Once the solution works for the hand example, we should also test it with additional sets of data to be sure that the solution works for other valid sets of data.

CHAPTER SUMMARY

A set of grand challenges was presented to illustrate some of the exciting and difficult problems that currently face engineers and scientists. Because the solutions to most engineering problems, including the grand challenges, will be by computer, we also presented a summary of the components of a computer system, from computer hardware to computer software. We also introduced a five-step problem-solving methodology that we will use to develop a computer solution to a problem. These five steps are as follows:

1. State the problem clearly.
2. Describe the input and output information.
3. Work the problem by hand (or with a calculator) for a simple set of data.
4. Develop an algorithm and convert it to a computer program.
5. Test the solution with a variety of data.

This process will be used throughout the text as we develop solutions to problems.

KEY TERMS

algorithm
ANSI C
arithmetic logic unit (ALU)
assembler
assembly language
binary
bug
central processing unit (CPU)
compiler
compile error
computer
computer-aided design (CAD)
database management tool
debug
debugger
decomposition outline
desktop publishing
electronic copy
execution
grand challenges
hardware
high-level language
I/O diagram
linking/loading
logic error

low-level language
machine language
mathematical tool
memory
microprocessor
network
object program
operating system
personal computer (PC)
problem-solving methodology
processor
program
real-time program
software
software life cycle
software maintenance
software prototype
software tool
source program
spreadsheet
supercomputer
syntax
utility
word processor
workstation

2

Courtesy of National Aeronautics and Space Administration.

GRAND CHALLENGE:
Vehicle Performance

Wind tunnels are test chambers built to generate precise wind speeds. Accurate scale models of new aircraft can be mounted on force-measuring supports in the test chamber. Measurements of the forces on the model can then be made at many different wind speeds and angles. Some wind tunnels operate at hypersonic velocities, generating wind speeds of thousands of miles per hour. The sizes of wind tunnel test sections vary from a few inches across to sizes large enough to accommodate a jet fighter. At the completion of a wind tunnel test series, many sets of data have been collected, which can be used to determine the lift, drag, and other aerodynamic performance characteristics of a new aircraft at its various operating speeds and positions.

Simple C Programs

OBJECTIVES

In this chapter, we outline the structure of a simple C program that defines variables, performs computations, and prints the results. We then present the syntax and the semantics for the C statements that define and initialize constants and variables, that compute new values using simple arithmetic operations, that read user-supplied information from the keyboard during the execution of a program, and that print information on the screen. Additional functions are presented for most of the numerical computations commonly used to solve engineering problems. With these C statements and functions, we can write complete programs.

2.1   Program Structure

General structure

In this section we analyze the structure of a specific C program, and then we present the **general structure** of a C program. The program below was first introduced in Chapter 1; it computes and prints the distance between two points.

```
/*-----------------------------------------------------*/
/*  Program chapter1_1                                 */
/*                                                     */
/*  This program computes the                          */
/*  distance between two points.                       */

#include <stdio.h>
#include <stdlib.h>
#include <math.h>

main()
{
    /*  Declare and initialize variables.  */
    double x1=1, y1=5, x2=4, y2=7,
           side_1, side_2, distance;

    /*  Compute sides of a right triangle.  */
    side_1 = x2 - x1;
    side_2 = y2 - y1;
    distance = sqrt(side_1*side_1 + side_2*side_2);

    /*  Print distance.  */
    printf("The distance between the two points is "
           "%5.2f \n",distance);

    /*  Exit program.  */
    return EXIT_SUCCESS;
}
/*-----------------------------------------------------*/
```

We now briefly discuss the statements in this specific example; each of the statements is discussed in detail in later sections of this chapter.

Comments

The first five lines of this program contain **comments** that give the program a name (`chapter1_1`) and define its purpose:

```
/*-----------------------------------------------------*/
/*  Program chapter1_1                                 */
/*                                                     */
/*  This program computes the                          */
/*  distance between two points.                       */
```

Comments begin with the characters /* and end with the characters */. A comment can be on a line by itself, or it can be on the same line as a command; a comment can also extend over several lines. Each of the comment lines here is a separate comment because each line begins with /* and ends with */. *Comments are optional, but good style requires that comments be used throughout a program to*

Style

improve its readability and to document the computations. In the text programs, we always use initial comments to give a name to the program and to describe the general purpose of the program; additional explanation comments are also included throughout the program. ANSI C allows comments and statements to begin anywhere on a line; we begin the initial comments of a program in the first column.

Preprocessor directives give instructions to the compiler that are performed before the program is compiled. The most common directive inserts additional statements in the program; it contains the characters **#include** followed by the name of the file containing the additional statements. This program contains the following three preprocessor directives:

```
#include <stdio.h>
#include <stdlib.h>
#include <math.h>
```

These directives specify that statements in the files **stdio.h**, **stdlib.h**, and **math.h** should be inserted in place of these three statements before the program is executed. The **<** and **>** characters around the file names indicate that the files are included with the **Standard C library**; this library is contained in the files that accompany an ANSI C compiler. The **stdio.h** file contains information related to the output statement used in this program, the **stdlib.h** file contains a constant we will use in exiting the program, and the **math.h** file contains information related to the function used in this program to compute the square root of a value. The **h** extension on these file names specifies that they are header files; more information on header files is included later in this chapter and in Chapter 4. Preprocessor directives are generally included after the initial comments describing the program's purpose.

Every C program contains a function named **main**. The body of the function is enclosed by braces, **{ }**. In order to identify the body of the function easily, we place these braces on lines by themselves. Thus, the two lines following the processor directives specify the beginning of the **main** function:

```
main()
{
```

The **main** function contains two types of commands: declarations and statements. The **declarations** define the memory locations that will be used by the statements; therefore, the declarations must precede the statements. The declarations may or may not give **initial values** to be stored in the memory locations. A comment precedes the declaration statement in this program:

```
/* Declare and initialize variables. */
double x1=1, y1=5, x2=4, y2=7,
       side_1, side_2, distance;
```

These declarations specify that the program will use seven variables named **x1**, **y1**, **x2**, **y2**, **side_1**, **side_2**, and **distance**. The term **double** indicates that the variables will store **double-precision floating-point** values. These variables can store

Preprocessor directives

Standard C library

Declarations

values, such as 12.5 and −0.0005, with many digits of precision. In addition, this statement specifies that **x1** should be initialized (given an initial value) to the value 1, **y1** should be initialized to the value 5, **x2** should be initialized to the value 4, and **y2** should be initialized to the value 7. The initial values of **side_1**, **side_2**, and **distance** are not specified and should not be assumed to be initialized to zero.

Style

Because the declaration was too long for one line, we split it over two lines; the indenting of the second line indicates that it is a continuation of the previous line.

The **statements** that specify the operations to be performed in the example program are the following:

```
/* Compute sides of a right triangle.  */
side_1 = x2 - x1;
side_2 = y2 - y1;
distance = sqrt(side_1*side_1 + side_2*side_2);

/* Print distance.  */
printf("The distance between the two points is "
       "%5.2f \n",distance);
```

These statements compute the lengths of the two sides of the right triangle formed by two points (see Figure 1.4, page 17) and then compute the length of the hypotenuse of the right triangle. The details of the syntax of these statements are discussed later in the chapter. After computing the distance, it is printed with the **printf** statement. This output statement is too long for a single line, so we separate the statement into two lines; the indenting of the second line again indicates that it is a continuation of the previous line. Additional comments were used to explain the computations and the output statement. Also, note that the declarations and statements must end with a semicolon.

To exit the program, we use a **return** statement. The constant **EXIT_SUCCESS** is defined in the **stdlib.h** file and indicates a successful exit from the program.

```
/* Exit program.  */
return EXIT_SUCCESS;
```

The use of a **return** statement at the end of the **main** function is optional in ANSI C; we use it for documentation purposes.

The body of the **main** function ends with the right brace on a line by itself and another comment line to delineate the end of the **main** function.

```
}
/*-------------------------------------------------------*/
```

Style

Note that we have also included blank lines (also called white space) in the program to separate the different components. *These blank lines make a program more readable and easier to modify.* The declarations and statements within the **main** function were indented three columns in order to show the structure of the program. This spacing provides a consistent style and makes our programs easier to read.

Now that we have closely examined the C program from Chapter 1, we can compare its structure to the **general form** of a C program:

```
preprocessing directives
main()
{
        declarations;
        statements;
}
```

This structure is evident in the programs developed in this chapter and in the chapters that follow.

2.2   Constants and Variables

Identifier

Constants and variables represent values that we use in our programs. **Constants** are specific values, such as 2, 3.1416, or -1.5, that we include in the C statements; **variables** are memory locations that are assigned a name or **identifier**. The identifier is used to reference the value stored in the memory location. A useful analogy for a memory location and its corresponding identifier is a mailbox that is associated with the name of an individual; the memory location (or mailbox) then contains a value. The following diagram shows the variables, their identifiers, and their initial values after the following declaration statement from program `chapter1_1`:

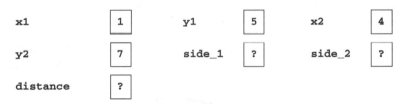

```
double x1=1, y1=5, x2=4, y2=7,
        side_1, side_2, distance;
```

| x1 | 1 | | y1 | 5 | | x2 | 4 |

| y2 | 7 | | side_1 | ? | | side_2 | ? |

| distance | ? |

Memory snapshot

The values of variables that were not given initial values are unspecified and are indicated with a question mark. Sometimes these values are called **garbage values** because they are values left in memory from the previous program. A diagram that shows a variable along with its identifier and its value is called a **memory snapshot** because it shows the contents of a memory location at a specified point in the execution of a program. The preceding memory snapshot shows the variables and their contents as specified by the declaration statement. We frequently use memory snapshots to show the contents of variables both before and after a statement is executed in order to show its effect.

The rules for selecting a valid identifier are summarized in this list:

• An identifier must begin with an alphabetic character or the underscore character _.

• Alphabetic characters in an identifier can be lowercase or uppercase.

• An identifier can contain digits, but not as the first character.

- An identifier can be of any length, but the first 31 characters of the identifier must be unique.

C is **case sensitive**, so uppercase letters are different from lowercase letters; thus `Total`, `TOTAL`, and `total` represent three different variables. Also, the variable `distance_in_miles_from_earth_to_mars` would not be distinguished from `distance_in_miles_from_earth_to_venus` because the first 31 characters are the same. C also includes **keywords** with special meanings to the C compiler that cannot be used for identifiers; a complete list is given in Table 2.1.

Examples of valid identifiers are `distance`, `x_1`, `X_Sum`, `average_measurement`, and `initial_time`. Examples of invalid identifiers are `1x` (begins with a digit), `minimum-x` (contains an invalid character −), `I/O` (contains an invalid character /), `switch` (a keyword), `$sum` (contains an invalid character $), and `rate%` (contains an invalid character %).

Style

An identifier name should be carefully selected so that it reflects the contents of the variable. *If possible, the name should also indicate the units of measurement.* For example, if a variable represents a temperature measurement in degrees Fahrenheit, use an identifier such as `temp_F` or `degrees_F`. If a variable represents an angle, name it `theta_rad` to indicate that the angle is measured in radians or `theta_deg` to indicate that the angle is measured in degrees.

The declarations at the beginning of the `main` function (and also at the beginning of other C functions that we write) must not only include all identifiers of the variables that we plan to use in our program, but must also specify the types of values that will be stored in the variables. These data types are presented after a discussion on scientific notation.

Practice!

Determine which of the following names are valid identifiers. If a name is not a valid identifier, give the reason that it is not acceptable, and suggest a valid replacement.

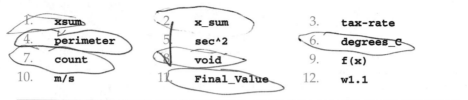

1.	xsum	2.	x_sum	3.	tax-rate
4.	perimeter	5.	sec^2	6.	degrees_C
7.	count	8.	void	9.	f(x)
10.	m/s	11.	Final_Value	12.	w1.1

SCIENTIFIC NOTATION

Floating-point value

A **floating-point value** is one that can represent both integer and noninteger values, such as 2.5, −0.004, and 15.0. A floating-point value expressed in **scientific notation** is rewritten as a mantissa times a power of ten, where the **mantissa** has an absolute value greater than or equal to 1.0 and less than 10.0. For example, in scientific notation, 25.6 is written as 2.56×10^1, −0.004 is written as -4.0×10^{-3},

---

TABLE 2.1 Keywords

auto	double	int	struct
break	else	long	switch
case	enum	register	typedef
char	extern	return	union
const	float	short	unsigned
continue	for	signed	void
default	goto	sizeof	volatile
do	if	static	while

---

and 1.5 is written as 1.5×10^0. In **exponential notation**, the letter e is used to separate the mantissa from the exponent of the power of ten. Thus, in exponential notation, 25.6 is written as 2.56e1, -0.004 is written as $-4.0e-3$, and 1.5 is written as 1.5e0.

Precision

The number of digits allowed by the computer for the decimal portion of the mantissa determines the **precision** or accuracy, and the number of digits allowed for the exponent determines the **range**. Thus, values with one digit of accuracy and an exponent range of -8 to 7 could include values such as 2.3×10^5 (230,000) and 5.9×10^{-8} (0.000000059). This precision and exponent range would not be sufficient for many of the types of values that we use in engineering problem solutions. For example, the distance in miles from Mars to the sun, with seven digits of precision, is 141,517,510 or 1.4151751×10^8; to represent this value we would need at least seven digits of accuracy and an exponent range that included the integer 8.

Practice!

In problems 1–4, express the value in scientific notation. Specify the number of digits of precision needed to represent each value.

1. 35.004
2. 0.00042
3. -0.0999
4. 10,000,002.8

Handwritten answers:
1) 3.5004×10^1
2) 4.2×10^{-4}
3) -9.9×10^{-4}
4) 1.0000028×10^7

In problems 5–8, express the value in floating-point notation.

5. 1.03e-5
6. -1.05e5
7. -3.552e6
8. 6.67e-4

Handwritten answers:
5) .0000103
6) -105000.0
7) -3552000.0
8) .000667

NUMERIC DATA TYPES

Numeric data types are used to specify the types of numbers that will be contained in variables. In C, numeric values are either integers or floating-point values, as shown in Figure 2.1. Nonnumeric data types (such as characters) are discussed in Chapter 6.

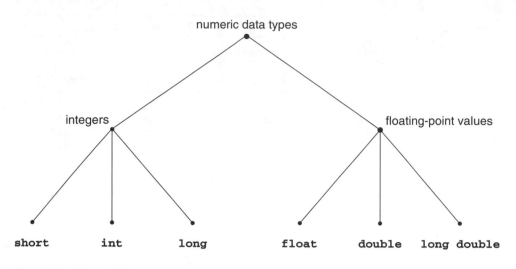

Figure 2.1   Numeric data types

Type specifier   The **type specifiers** for signed integers are **short**, **int**, and **long**, for short integer, integer, and long integer, respectively. The specific ranges of values are **system dependent**, which means that the ranges can vary from one system to another. On many systems, the short integer and the integer data types range from −32,768 to 32,767, and the long integer type often represents values from −2,147,483,648 to 2,147,483,647. (The unusual limits, such as 32,767 and 2,147,483,647, relate to conversions of binary values to decimal values.) C also allows an **unsigned** qualifier to be added to integer specifiers, where an unsigned integer represents only positive values. Signed and unsigned integers can represent the same number of values, but the ranges are different. For example, if an **unsigned short** has the range of values from 0 to 65,535, then a **short** integer has the range of values from −32,768 to 32,767; both variables can represent a total of 65,536 values.

The type specifiers for floating-point values are **float** (single-precision), **double** (double-precision), and **long double** (extended precision). The following statement from program **chapter1_1** thus defines seven variables that all contain double-precision floating-point values:

```
double x1=1, y1=5, x2=4, y2=7,
       side_1, side_2, distance;
```

The difference between the **float**, **double**, and **long double** types relates to the precision (or accuracy) and the range of the values represented. The precision and range are **system-dependent**. Table 2.2 contains precision and range information for integers and floating-point values used by the Borland C++ compiler, which can be used to run C programs as well as C++ programs. (C++ is an extension of C.) On most systems, a **double** data type stores about twice as many decimal digits of precision as are stored with a **float** data type. In addition, a **double** value will have a wider range of exponent values than a

TABLE 2.2 Example Data Type Limits*	
Integers	
`short`	maximum = 32,767
`int`	maximum = 32,767
`long`	maximum = 2,147,483,647
Floating Point	
`float`	6 digits of precision maximum exponent = 38 maximum value = 3.402823e + 38
`double`	15 digits of precision maximum exponent = 308 maximum value = 1.797693e + 308
`long double`	19 digits of precision maximum exponent = 4932 maximum value = 1.189731e + 4932

*Borland Turbo C++ 3.1 Compiler

`float` value. The `long double` value may have more precision and a still wider exponent range, but this is again system dependent. A floating-point constant, such as 2.3, is assumed to be a `double` constant. To specify a `float` constant or a `long double` constant, the letter (or suffix) `F` or `L` must be appended to the constant. Thus, `2.3F` and `2.3L` represent a `float` constant and a `long double` constant, respectively.

SYMBOLIC CONSTANTS

Style

A **symbolic constant** is defined with a preprocessor directive that assigns an identifier to the constant. The directive can appear anywhere in a C program; the compiler will replace each occurrence of the directive identifier with the constant value in all statements that follow the directive. *Engineering constants such as π or the acceleration of gravity are good candidates for symbolic constants.* For example, consider the following preprocessing directive to assign the value 3.141593 to the variable PI with the following statement:

```
#define PI 3.141593
```

Statements that need to use the value of π would then use the symbolic constant identifier instead of 3.141593, as illustrated in this statement

```
area = PI*radius*radius;
```

which computes the area of a circle.

Style

Symbolic constants are usually defined with uppercase identifiers (as in PI *instead of* pi*) to indicate that they are symbolic constants, and of course, the identifiers should be selected so that they are easy to remember.* Finally, only one symbolic constant can be defined in a directive; if several symbolic constants are desired, several separate directives are required. Note that pre-processor directives, which include the #define statement, do not end with a semicolon.

In the next section we discuss C statements that allow us to assign values to variables. These assignment statements could be used to assign constant values to variables, but we will see later that there are some special advantages to using symbolic constants in many cases.

Practice!

Give preprocessor directives to assign symbolic constants for these constants.

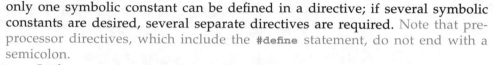

1. speed of light, $c = 2.99792 \times 10^8$ m/s   #define light_ SPEED   2.997920 8
2. charge of an electron, $e = 1.602177 \times 10^{-19}$ C
3. acceleration of gravity, $g = 9.8$ m/s^2
4. acceleration of gravity, $g = 32$ ft/s^2
5. radius of the moon, $r = 1.74 \times 10^6$m

2.3   Assignment Statements

An **assignment statement** is used to assign a value to an identifier. The general form of the assignment statement is

        identifier = expression;

Expression

where an **expression** can be a constant, another variable, or the result of an opera-tion. Consider the following two sets of statements that declare and give values to the variables **sum** and **x1**:

```
double sum=10.5;          double sum;
int x1=3;                 int x1;
                          ...
                          sum = 10.5;
                          x1 = 3;
```

After either set of statements is executed, the value of sum is 10.5, and the value of x1 is 3, as shown in the following memory snapshot.

        sum | 10.5 | x1 | 3 |

The set of statements on the left define and initialize the variables at the same time; the assignment statements on the right could be used at any point in the program and thus may be used to change (as opposed to initialize) the values in variables.

Multiple assignment

Multiple assignments are also allowed in C, as in the following statement, which assigns a value of zero to each of the variables **x**, **y**, and **z**:

```
x = y = z = 0;
```

Multiple assignments are discussed further at the end of this section.

We can also assign a value from one variable to another with an assignment statement:

```
rate = state_tax;
```

The equal sign should be read as "is assigned the value of"; thus, this statement is "**rate** is assigned the value of **state_tax**." If **state_tax** contains the value 0.06, then **rate** also contains the value 0.06 after the statement is executed; the value in **state_tax** is not changed. Thus, the memory snapshots before and after this statement is executed are the following:

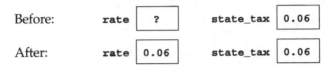

If we assign a value to a variable that has a different data type, then a conversion must occur during the execution of the statement. Sometimes the conversion can result in information being lost. For example, consider the following declaration and assignment statement:

```
int a;
...
a = 12.8;
```

Because **a** is defined to be an integer, it cannot store a value with a nonzero decimal portion. Therefore, in this case, the memory snapshot after executing the assignment statement is the following:

```
a    | 12 |
```

Numeric conversion

To determine if a **numeric conversion** will work properly, we use the following order, which is from high to low:

high: long double
         double
         float
         long integer
         integer
low: short integer

If a value is moved to a data type that is higher in order, no information will be lost; if a value is moved to a data type that is lower in order, information may be lost. Thus, moving an integer to a double will work properly, but moving a float to an integer may result in the loss of some information or in an incorrect result. In general, use only assignments that do not cause potential conversion problems. (Unsigned integers were not included in the list because errors can occur in both directions.)

ARITHMETIC OPERATORS

An assignment statement can be used to assign the result of an arithmetic operation to a variable, as shown in this statement, which computes the area of a square

```
area_square = side*side;
```

where * is used to indicate multiplication. The symbols + and - are used to indicate addition and subtraction, and the symbol / is used for division. Thus, each of the following statements is a valid computation for the area of a triangle:

```
area_triangle = 0.5*base*height;
```

```
area_triangle = (base*height)/2;
```

The use of parentheses in the second statement is not required but is used for readability.

Consider this assignment statement:

```
x = x + 1;
```

In algebra, this statement is invalid because a value cannot be equal to itself plus 1. However, this assignment statement should not be read as an equality; instead, it should be read as "x is assigned the value of x plus 1." With this interpretation, the statement indicates that the value stored in the variable x is incremented by 1. Thus, if the value of x is 5 before this statement is executed, then the value of x will be 6 after the statement is executed.

Modulus

C also includes a **modulus** operator %, which is used to compute the remainder in a division between two integers. For example, 5%2 is equal to 1, 6%3 is equal to 0, and 2%7 is equal to 2. (The quotient of 2/7 is zero with a remainder of 2.) If a and b are integers, then the expression a/b computes the integer quotient, whereas the expression a%b computes the integer remainder. Thus, if a is equal to 9 and b is equal to 4, the value of a/b is 2, and the value of a%b is 1. An execution error occurs if the value of b is equal to zero in either a/b or a%b because the computer cannot perform **division by zero**. If either of the integer values in a and b is negative, the results of a/b and a%b are system dependent.

The modulus operator is useful in determining if an integer is a multiple of another number. For example, if a%2 is equal to zero, then a is even; otherwise a is odd. If **a%5** is equal to zero, then **a** is a multiple of 5. We will use the modulus operator frequently in the development of engineering solutions.

The five operators (**+, -, *, /, %**) discussed in the previous paragraphs are **binary operators**—operators that operate on two values. C also includes **unary operators**—operators that operate on a single value. For example, plus and minus signs can be unary operators when they are used in an expression such as **-x**.

The result of a binary operation with values of the same type is another value of the same type. For example, if **a** and **b** are **double** values, then the result of **a/b** is also a **double** value. Similarly, if **a** and **b** are integers, then the result of **a/b** is also an integer. However, an integer division can sometimes produce unexpected results because any decimal portion of the integer division is dropped; the result is a **truncated result**, not a rounded result. Thus, **5/3** is equal to 1, and **3/6** is equal to 0.

Truncated result

An operation between values with different types is a **mixed operation**. Before the operation is performed, the value with the lower type is converted or promoted to the higher type (as discussed in conversions within assignment statements on page 31); thus, the operation is performed with values of the same type. For example, if an operation is specified between an integer and a **float**, the integer will be converted to a **float** before the operation is performed; the result will be a **float**.

Suppose that we want to compute the average of a set of integers. If the sum and the count of the integers have been stored in the integer variables **sum** and **count**, it would seem that the following statements should correctly compute the average:

```
int sum, count;
float average;
...
average = sum/count;
```

Cast operator

However, the division between these two integers gives an integer result that is then converted to a **float** value. Thus, if **sum** is 18 and **count** is 5, the value of **average** is 3.0, not 3.6. To compute this sum correctly, we use a **cast operator**—a unary operator that allows us to specify a type change in the value before the next computation. In this example, the cast (**float**) is applied to **sum**:

```
average = (float)sum/count;
```

The value of **sum** is converted to a **float** value before the division is performed. The division is then a mixed operation between a **float** value and an integer, so the value of **count** is converted to a **float** value. The result of the division is then a **float** value that is stored in **average**. If the value of **sum** is 18 and the value of **count** is 5, the value of **average** is now correctly computed to be 3.6. Note that the cast operator affects only the value used in the computation; it does not change the value stored in the variable **sum**.

Practice!

Give the value computed by each of the following sets of statements.

1.
```
int a=27, b=6, c;
...
c = b%a;
```

2.
```
int a=27, b=6;
float c;
...
c = a/(float)b;
```

3.
```
int a;
float b=6, c = 18.6;
...
a = c/b;
```

4.
```
int b=6;
float a, c=18.6;
...
a = (int)c/b;
```

PRIORITY OF OPERATORS

Precedence

In an expression that contains more than one arithmetic operator, we need to be concerned about the order in which the operations are performed. Table 2.3 contains the **precedence** of the arithmetic operators, which matches the standard algebraic precedence. Operations within parentheses are always evaluated first; if the parentheses are nested, the operations within the innermost parentheses are evaluated first. Unary operators are evaluated before the binary operators *, /, and %. Binary addition and subtraction are evaluated last. If there are several operators of the same precedence level in an expression, the variables or constants are grouped (or associated) with the operators in a specific order, as specified in Table 2.3. For example, consider the following expression:

```
a*b + b/c*d
```

Associativity

Because multiplication and division have the same precedence level, and because the **associativity** (the order for grouping the operations) is from left to right, this expression will be evaluated as if it contained the following:

```
(a*b) + ((b/c)*d)
```

The precedence order does not specify whether `a*b` is evaluated before `(b/c)*d`; the order of evaluation of these terms is system dependent.

Style

The spacing within an arithmetic expression is a style issue. Some people prefer to put spaces around each operator. We prefer to put spaces around only binary addition and subtraction because they are evaluated last. *Choose the spacing style that you prefer; then use it consistently.*

Assume that we want to compute the area of a trapezoid and that we have declared four **double** variables: **base**, **height_1**, **height_2**, and **area**. Assume further that the variables **base**, **height_1**, and **height_2** already have values. A statement to correctly compute the area of the trapezoid is

```
area = 0.5*base*(height_1 + height_2);
```

TABLE 2.3 Precedence of Arithmetic Operators		
Precedence	Operator	Associativity
1	parentheses: ( )	innermost first
2	unary operators: + - (type)	right to left
3	binary operators: * / %	left to right
4	binary operators: + -	left to right

Suppose that we omitted the parentheses in the expression

```
area = 0.5*base*height_1 + height_2;
```

The statement would be executed as if it were this statement:

```
area = ((0.5*base)*height_1) + height_2;
```

Note that although an incorrect answer has been computed, there is no error message to alert us to the error. Therefore, it is important to be very careful when converting expressions into C. In general, use parentheses to indicate the order of operations in a complicated expression to avoid confusion and to be sure that the expression is evaluated in the manner desired.

You may have noticed that there is not an operator for an exponentiation operation to compute values such as x^4. A special mathematical function will be discussed later in this chapter to perform exponentiations. Of course, exponentiations with integer exponents, such as a^2, can be computed with repeated multiplications, as in a*a.

The evaluation of long expressions should be broken into several statements. For example, consider the following equation:

$$f = \frac{x^3 - 2x^2 + x - 6.3}{x^2 + 0.05005x - 3.14}$$

If we try to evaluate the expression in one statement, it becomes too long to be easily read:

```
f = (x*x*x - 2*x*x + x - 6.3)/(x*x + 0.05005*x - 3.14);
```

We could break the statement into two lines:

```
f = (x*x*x - 2*x*x + x - 6.3)/
    (x*x + 0.05005*x - 3.14);
```

Another solution is to compute the numerator and denominator separately:

```
numerator = x*x*x - 2*x*x + x - 6.3;
denominator = x*x + 0.05005*x - 3.14;
f = numerator/denominator;
```

The variables **x, numerator, denominator,** and **f** must be floating-point variables in order to compute the correct value of **f**.

Practice!

In problems 1–2 give C statements to compute the indicated values. Assume that the identifiers in the expressions have been defined as **double** variables and have also been assigned appropriate values. Use the following constant:

acceleration of gravity: $g = 9.80665 \text{ m/s}^2$

1. Tension in a cord:

$$\text{tension} = \frac{2m_1m_2}{m_1 + m_2} \cdot g$$

2. Fluid pressure at the end of a pipe:

$$P_2 = P_1 + \frac{\rho v_2{}^2(A_2{}^2 - A_1{}^2)}{2A_1{}^2}$$

In problems 3–4, give the mathematical equations computed by the C statements. Assume that the following symbolic constants have been defined, where the units of **G** are $\text{m}^3/(\text{kg} \cdot \text{s}^2)$:

```
#define PI 3.141593
#define G 6.67259e-11
```

3. Centripetal acceleration:

```
centripetal = 4*PI*PI*r/(T*T);
```

4. Change in potential energy:

```
change = G*M_E*m*(1/R_E - 1/(R_E + h));
```

OVERFLOW AND UNDERFLOW

The values stored in a computer have a wide range of allowed values. However, if the result of a computation exceeds the range of allowed values, an error occurs. For example, assume that the exponent range of a floating point value is from -38 to 38. This range should accommodate most computations, but it is possible for the results of an expression to be outside of this range. For example, suppose that we execute the following commands:

```
x = 2.5e30;
y = 1.0e30;
z = x*y;
```

The values of **x** and **y** are within the allowable range. However, the value of **z** should be 2.5e60, but this value exceeds the range. This error is called **exponent overflow** because the exponent of the result of an arithmetic operation is too large to store in the memory assigned to the variable. The action generated by an exponent overflow is system dependent.

Exponent underflow is a similar error caused by the exponent of the result of an arithmetic operation being too small to store in the memory assigned to the variable. Using the same allowable range as in the previous example, we obtain an exponent underflow with the following commands:

```
x = 2.5e-30;
y = 1.0e30;
z = x/y;
```

Again, the values of **x** and **y** are within the allowable range, but the value of **z** should be 2.5e−60. Because the exponent is less than the minimum value allowed, we have caused an exponent underflow. Again the action generated by an exponent underflow is system dependent; on some systems, the result of an operation with exponent underflow is set to zero.

INCREMENT AND DECREMENT OPERATORS

The C language contains unary operators for incrementing and decrementing variables; these operators cannot be used with constants or expressions. The increment operator ++ and the decrement operator -- can be applied either in a **prefix** position (before the identifier) as in **++count**, or in a **postfix** position (after the identifier) as in **count++**. If an increment or decrement operator is used by itself, it is equivalent to an assignment statement that increments or decrements the variable. Thus, the statement

```
y--;
```

is equal to this statement:

```
y = y - 1;
```

If the increment or decrement operator is used in an expression, the expression must be evaluated carefully. If the increment or decrement operator is in a prefix position, the identifier is modified, and the new value is used in evaluating the rest of the expression. If the increment or decrement operator is in a postfix position, the old value of the identifier is used to evaluate the rest of the expression, and then the identifier is modified. Thus, the execution of this statement

```
w = ++x - y;
```
(2.1)

is equivalent to the execution of this pair of statements:

```
x = x + 1;
w = x - y;
```

Similarly, this statement

```
w = x++ - y;
```
(2.2)

is equivalent to this pair of statements:

```
w = x - y;
x = x + 1;
```

When executing either (2.1) or (2.2), if we assume that the value of x is equal to 5 and the value of y is equal to 3, then the value of x increases to 6. However, after executing (2.1), the value of w is 3; but after executing (2.2), the value of w is 2.

The increment and decrement operators have the same precedence as the other unary operators. If several unary operators are in an expression, they are associated from right to left.

ABBREVIATED ASSIGNMENT OPERATORS

C allows simple assignment statements to be abbreviated. For example, each pair of statements contains equivalent statements:

```
x = x + 3;
x += 3;

sum = sum + x;
sum += x;

d = d/4.5;
d /= 4.5;

r = r%2;
r %= 2;
```

In fact, any statement of this form

identifier = identifier operator expression;

can be written in this form:

> identifier operator = expression;

Abbreviated assignment statements are usually used because they are shorter. Earlier in this section, we used the following **multiple-assignment** statement:

```
x = y = z = 0;
```

The interpretation of this statement is clear, but the interpretation of the following statement is not as evident:

```
a = b += c + d;
```

To evaluate this properly, we use Table 2.4, which indicates that the assignment operators are evaluated last, and their associativity is right to left. Thus, the statement is equivalent to the following:

```
a = (b += (c + d));
```

If we replace the abbreviated forms with the longer forms of the operations, we have

```
a = (b = b + (c + d));
```

or

```
b = b + (c + d);
a = b;
```

Evaluating this statement was good practice with the precedence/associativity table, but in general, statements used in a program should be more readable. Therefore, using abbreviated assignment statements in a multiple assignment statement is not recommended. *Also, note that the spacing conventions that we use insert spaces around abbreviated operators and multiple assignment operators because these operators are evaluated after the arithmetic operators.*

Style

Practice!

Give a memory snapshot after each statement is executed, assuming that **x** is equal to 2 and that **y** is equal to 4 before the statement is executed. Also, assume that all the variables are integers.

1. `z = x++ * y;`   2. `z = ++x * y;`
3. `x += y;`   4. `y %= x;`

	TABLE 2.4 Precedence of Arithmetic and Assignment Operators	
Precedence	Operator	Associativity
1	parentheses: ( )	innermost first
2	unary operators: + - ++ --(type)	right to left
3	binary operators: * / %	left to right
4	binary operators: + -	left to right
5	assignment operators: = += -= *= /= %=	right to left

2.4   Standard Input and Output

We have discussed statements for declaring variables and then using the variables to compute new values. We now present a statement that allows us to print the new values computed. In addition, we also discuss a statement that allows us to enter values from the keyboard when the program is executed. To use either of these statements in a program, we must include the following preprocessor directive:

```
#include <stdio.h>
```

This directive gives the compiler the information that it needs to check references to the input/output functions in the Standard C library.

printf FUNCTION

The **printf** function allows us to print values and explanatory text to the screen. For example, consider the following statement that prints the value of a **double** variable named **angle** along with the corresponding units:

```
printf("Angle = %f radians \n",angle);
```

Conversion specifier

This **printf** statement contains two arguments—a control string and an identifier to specify the value to be printed. A **control string** is enclosed in double quotation marks and can contain text or conversion specifiers or both. A **conversion specifier** describes the format to use in printing the value of a variable. In the previous example, the control string specifies that the characters **Angle =** are to be printed. The next group of characters (**%f**) represents a conversion specifier that indicates that a value is to be printed next, which will then be followed by the characters **radians**. The next combination of characters (**\n**) represents a **new line** indicator; it causes a skip to a new line on the screen after the information has been printed. The second argument in the **printf** statement is a variable **angle**; it is matched to the conversion specifier in the control string. Thus, the value in **angle** is printed according to the specification **%f** which will be explained later. If the value of **angle** is 2.84, the output generated by the previous statement is

```
Angle = 2.840000 radians
```

Now that we have analyzed a simple statement and its corresponding output, we are ready to look closer at the conversion specifiers.

To select a conversion specifier for a value to be printed, first select the correct type of specifier as indicated in Table 2.5. For example, to print a **short** or an **int**, use an **%i** (integer) or **%d** (decimal) specifier (either specifier gives the same results); and to print a **long**, use an **%li** or **%ld** specifier. To print a **float** or a **double**, use an **%f** (floating-point form), **%e** (exponential form, as in **2.3e+02**), or **%E** (exponential form, as in **2.3E+02**). The **%g** (general) specifier prints the value using an **%f** or **%e** specifier, depending on the size of the value; the **%G** specifier is the same as the **%g**, except that it prints the value using an **%f** or **%E** specifier.

Field width

After selecting the correct specifier, additional information can be added. A minimum **field width** can be specified, along with an optional precision that controls the number of characters printed. The field width and the **precision** can be used together or separately. If the precision is omitted, a default of 6 is used for the **%f** specifier. The decimal portion of a value is rounded to the specified precision; thus, the value 14.51678 will be printed as **14.52** if a **%.2f** specification is used. The specification **%5i** indicates that a **short** or an **int** is to be printed with a minimum field width of 5. The field width will be increased if necessary to print the corresponding value. If the field width specifies more positions than are needed for the value, the value is **right-justified**, which means that the extra positions are filled with blanks on the left of the value. To **left-justify** a value, a minus sign is inserted before the field width, as in **%-8i**. If a plus sign is inserted before the field width, as in **%+6f**, a sign will always be printed with the value.

The list on the next page shows several conversion specifiers and the resulting output fields for a given value; the character ♭ is used to indicate the location of

TABLE 2.5 Numeric Conversion Specifiers for Output Statements		
Variable Type	Output Type	Specifier
Integer Values		
short, int	int	%i, %d
int	short	%hi, %hd
long	long	%li, %ld
int	unsigned int	%u
int	unsigned short	%hu
long	unsigned long	%lu
Floating-Point Values		
float, double	double	%f, %e, %E, %g, %G
long double	long double	%Lf, %Le, %LE, %Lg, %LG

blanks within the field. In these examples, assume that the corresponding integer value is -145:

Specifier	Value Printed
%i	-145
%4d	-145
%3i	-145
%6i	bb-145
%-6i	-145bb

The next list shows several conversion specifiers and the resulting output fields for the **double** value 157.8926:

Specifier	Value Printed
%f	157.892600
%6.2f	157.89
%+8.2f	b+157.89
%7.5f	157.89260
%e	1.578926e+02
%.3E	1.579E+02
%g	157.893

Note the rounding that occurred with the last two specifiers.

If a control argument contains three conversion specifiers, three corresponding identifiers or expressions would need to follow the control string, as in this statement:

```
printf("Results: x = %5.2f, y = %5.2f, z = %5.2f",
       x, y, z+3);
```

An example output from this statement is

```
Results: x =    4.52, y =   0.15, z = -1.34
```

Note that the last conversion specifier matches to an arithmetic expression instead of a simple variable.

Escape character

The backslash (\) is called an **escape character** when it is used in a control string. The compiler combines it with the character that follows it and then attaches a special meaning to the combination of characters. For example, we have already seen that \n represents a skip to a new line. In addition, the sequence \\ is used to insert a single backslash in a control string, and the sequence \" will insert a double quote in a control string. Thus, the output of this statement

```
printf("\"The End.\"\n");
```

is a line containing

```
"The End."
```

The other escape sequences recognized by C are listed below:

Sequence	Character Represented
\a	alert (bell) character
\b	backspace
\f	formfeed
\n	newline
\r	carriage return
\t	horizontal tab
\v	vertical tab
\\	backslash
\?	question mark
\'	single quote
\"	double quote

If a `printf` statement is long, you should split it into two lines. In general, long lines should be split at a point that preserves readability. However, to split text that is contained in quotation marks, you should split the text into two separate pieces of text, each in its own set of quotation marks. The following statements show several different ways to correctly separate a statement:

```
printf("The distance between the points is %5.2f \n",
       distance);

printf("The distance between the points is"
       " %5.2f \n",distance);

printf("The distance between the "
       "points is %5.2f \n",distance);
```

Style

Conversion specifiers can be used to make the output of your program readable and usable. *For engineering values, it is also very important to include the corresponding units in the output along with the numerical values.*

Although the purpose of the `printf` function is to print information, it also returns a value that represents the number of characters printed.

Practice!

Assume that the integer variable **sum** contains the value 150 and that the **double** variable **average** contains the value 12.368. Show the output line (or lines) generated by the following statements.

1. `printf("Sum = %4i \n Average = %8.4f \n",sum,average);`

2. `printf("Sum and Average \n\n %d %.1f \n",sum,average);`

3. `printf("%7.2f is the average; \n",average);`
   `printf("%8d is the sum \n",sum);`

4.  ```
    printf("%7.2f is the average;",average);
    printf("%8d is the sum \n",sum);
    ```

scanf FUNCTION

The **scanf** function allows you to enter values from the keyboard when a program is executed. For example, suppose that a program computes the number of acres of new forest growth after a specified period of time elapses. If the time elapsed is a constant in the program, we would have to change the value of the constant and then recompile and reexecute the program to obtain the output for a different time period. Alternatively, if we use the **scanf** function to read the time period, we do not need to recompile the program; we only need to reexecute it and enter the desired time period from the keyboard.

The first argument of the **scanf** function is a control string that specifies the types of the variables whose values are to be entered from the keyboard. The type specifiers are shown in Table 2.6. Thus, for example, the specifiers for an integer variable are **%i** or **%d**; the specifiers for a **float** variable are **%f**, **%e**, and **%g**; and the specifiers for a **double** variable are **%lf**, **%le**, and **%lg**. It is very important to use a correct specifier. For example, errors will occur if you use an **%f** specifier to read the value for a **double** variable. The remaining arguments in the **scanf** function are memory locations that correspond to the specifiers in the control string. These memory locations are indicated with the **address operator &**. This operator is a unary operator that determines the memory address of the identifier with which it is associated. Thus, if the value to be entered through the keyboard is an integer that is to be stored in the variable **year**, we could use this statement to read the value:

Address operator

```
scanf("%i",&year);
```

The precedence level of the address operator is the same as the other unary operators; if there are several unary operators in the same statement, they are associated from right to left. A common error in the **scanf** statement is to omit the address operator for the identifiers.

If we wish to read more than one value from the keyboard, we can use statements such as the following:

```
scanf("%lf %lf",&distance,&velocity);
```

Style

When this statement is executed, the program will read two values from the keyboard and convert them into two **double** values. The values must be separated by at least one blank; they can be on the same line or on different lines. *In order to prompt the program user to enter the values, a scanf statement is usually preceded by a printf statement that describes the information that the user should enter from the keyboard:*

```
printf("Enter the distance(ft) and velocity(ft/s): \n");
scanf("%lf %lf",&distance,&velocity);
```
```

TABLE 2.6 Numeric Conversion Specifiers
for Input Statements

Variable Type	Specifier
Integer Values	
int	%i, %d
short	%hi, %hd
long int	%li, %ld
unsigned int	%u
unsigned short	%hu
unsigned long	%lu
Floating-Point Values	
float	%f, %e, %E, %g, %G
double	%lf, %le, %lE, %lg, %lG
long double	%Lf, %Le, %LE, %Lg, %LG

The control string of the **printf** statement ended with a new line specifier, so the values entered by the user will be on the line (or lines) following the prompt text. Thus, after the previous statements are executed and the user has responded to the prompt, the information on the screen might be

```
Enter the distance(ft) and velocity(ft/s):
10 15.5
```

If the characters entered by the user cannot be successfully converted to the types of values indicated by conversion specifiers in the **scanf** statement, the result is system dependent. These conversion errors include entering values such as 14.2 for integer values, including commas in large values, and forgetting to separate values with blanks.

Although the main purpose of the **scanf** function is to read input from the keyboard, the function also returns a value that is equal to the number of successful conversions. This value is used in programs in later chapters.

2.5   Mathematical Functions

Arithmetic expressions that solve engineering problems often require computations other than addition, subtraction, multiplication, and division. For example, many expressions require the use of exponentiation, logarithms, exponentials, and trigonometric functions. In this section we discuss the mathematical functions that are available in the Standard C library. The following preprocessor directive should be used in programs referencing the mathematical functions:

```
#include <math.h>
```

This directive specifies that information be added to the program to aid the compiler when it converts references to the mathematical functions in the Standard C library.

Before we discuss the rules relating to functions, we present a specific example. The following statement computes the sine of an angle **theta** and stores the result in the variable **b:**

```
b = sin(theta);
```

The **sin** function assumes that the argument is in radians. If the variable **theta** contains a value in degrees, we can convert the degrees to radians with a separate statement. (Recall that $180° = \pi$ radians.)

```
#define PI 3.141593
...
theta_rad = theta*PI/180;
b = sin(theta_rad);
```

The conversion can also be specified within the function reference:

```
b = sin(theta*PI/180);
```

Performing the conversion with a separate statement is usually preferable because it is easier to understand.

A function reference, such as **sin(theta)**, represents a single value. The parentheses following the function name contain the inputs to the function, which **Arguments** are called **parameters** or **arguments**. A function may contain no arguments, one argument, or many arguments, depending on its definition. If a function contains more than one argument, it is very important to list the arguments in the correct order. Some functions also require that the arguments be in specific units. For example, the trigonometric functions assume that arguments are in radians. Most of the mathematical functions assume that the arguments are **double** values; if a different type argument is used, it is converted to a **double** before the function is executed.

A function reference can also be part of the argument of another function reference. For example, the following statement computes the logarithm of the absolute value of **x:**

```
b = log(fabs(x));
```

When one function is used to compute the argument of another function, be sure to enclose the argument of each function in its own set of parentheses. This nesting of functions is also called **composition** of functions.

We now discuss several categories of functions that are commonly used in engineering computations. Other functions will be presented throughout the remaining chapters as we discuss relevant subjects. Tables of common functions are included on the last two pages of this book.

ELEMENTARY MATH FUNCTIONS

The elementary **math functions** include functions to perform a number of common computations, such as computing the absolute value of a number and the square root of a number. In addition, they also include a group of functions used to perform rounding. These functions assume that the type of each argument is **double**, and the functions all return a **double**; if an argument is not a **double**, a conversion will occur using the rules described in Section 2.3. We now list these functions with a brief description:

fabs(x)	This function computes the absolute value of **x**.
sqrt(x)	This function computes the square root of **x**, where $x \geq 0$.
pow(x,y)	This function is used for exponentiation and computes the value of **x** to the **y** power, or x^y. Errors occur if $x = 0$ and $y \leq 0$, or if $x < 0$ and **y** is not an integer.
ceil(x)	This function rounds **x** to the nearest integer toward ∞ (infinity). For example, **ceil(2.01)** is equal to 3.
floor(x)	This function rounds **x** to the nearest integer toward $-\infty$ (negative infinity). For example, **floor(2.01)** is equal to 2.
exp(x)	This function computes the value of e^x, where e is the base for natural logarithms, or approximately 2.718282.
log(x)	This function returns ln **x**, the natural logarithm of **x** to the base e. Errors occur if $x \leq 0$.
log10(x)	This function returns $\log_{10} x$, the common logarithm of **x** to the base 10. Errors occur if $x \leq 0$.

Remember that the logarithm of a negative value or zero does not exist; thus, an execution error occurs if you use a logarithm function with a negative or zero value for its argument.

An additional mathematical function that you may find useful is the **abs** function. This function computes the absolute value of an integer and returns an integer value. The header file containing information relative to this function is **stdlib.h**, and it should be included in programs referencing this function.

Practice!

Evaluate the following expressions:

1. **floor(-2.6)**
2. **ceil(-2.6)**
3. **pow(2,-3)**
4. **sqrt(floor(10.7))**

TRIGONOMETRIC FUNCTIONS

The **trigonometric functions** assume that all arguments are of type **double**, and they return values of type **double**. In addition, as previously stated, the trigonometric functions also assume that angles are represented in radians. To convert radians to degrees, or degrees to radians, use the following conversions, which use the fact that $180° = \pi$ radians:

```
#define PI 3.141593
...
angle_deg = angle_rad*(180/PI);
angle_rad = angle_deg*(PI/180);
```

The trigonometric functions are included in the Standard C library. A preprocessor directive including the information in **math.h** should be used with these functions. A brief summary of the functions follows:

sin(x)	This function computes the sine of **x**, where **x** is in radians.
cos(x)	This function computes the cosine of **x**, where **x** is in radians.
tan(x)	This function computes the tangent of **x**, where **x** is in radians.
asin(x)	This function computes the arcsine or inverse sine of **x**, where **x** must be in the range $[-1, 1]$. The function returns an angle in radians in the range $[-\pi/2, \pi/2]$.
acos(x)	This function computes the arccosine or inverse cosine of **x**, where **x** must be in the range $[-1, 1]$. The function returns an angle in radians in the range $[0, \pi]$.
atan(x)	This function computes the arctangent or inverse tangent of **x**. The function returns an angle in radians in the range $[-\pi/2, \pi/2]$.
atan2(y,x)	This function computes the arctangent or inverse tangent of the value y/x. The function returns an angle in radians in the range $[-\pi, \pi]$.

Note that the **atan** function always returns an angle in Quadrant I or IV, whereas the **atan2** function returns an angle that can be in any quadrant, depending on the signs of **x** and **y**. Thus, in many applications, the **atan2** function is preferred over the **atan** function.

Practice!

In problems 1–2, give assignment statements for computing the indicated values, assuming that the variables have been declared and given appropriate values. Also assume that the following declaration has been made:

```
#define g 9.8
```

1.   Length contraction:

$$\text{length} = k\sqrt{1 - \left(\frac{v}{c}\right)^2}$$

2.   Distance of the center of gravity from a reference plane in a hollow cylinder sector:

$$\text{center} = \frac{38.1972 \cdot (r^3 - s^3) \cdot \sin a}{(r^2 - s^2) \cdot a}$$

In problems 3–4, give the equations that correspond to the assignment statements.

3.   Range for a projectile:

```
range = (v0*v0/g)*sin(2*theta);
```

4.   Speed of a disk at the bottom of an incline:

```
v = sqrt(2*g*h/(1 + I/(m*pow(r,2))));
```

2.6   Problem Solving Applied: Velocity Computation

Unducted fan

In this section, we perform computations in an application related to the vehicle performance grand challenge. An advanced turboprop engine called the **unducted fan (UDF)** is one of the promising new propulsion technologies being developed for future transport aircraft. Turboprop engines, which have been in use for decades, combine the power and reliability of jet engines with the efficiency of propellers. They are a significant improvement over earlier piston-powered propeller engines. Their application has been limited to smaller commuter-type aircraft, however, because they are not as fast or powerful as the fanjet engines used on larger airliners. The UDF engine employs significant advancements in propeller technology, which narrow the performance gap between turboprops and fanjets. New materials, blade shapes, and higher rotation speeds enable UDF-powered aircraft to fly almost as fast as fanjets, and with greater fuel efficiency. The UDF is also significantly quieter than the conventional turboprop.

During a test flight of a UDF-powered aircraft, the test pilot has set the engine power level at 40,000 Newtons, which causes the 20,000-kg aircraft to attain a cruise speed of 180 m/s (meters/second). The engine throttles are then set to a power level of 60,000 Newtons, and the aircraft begins to accelerate. As the speed of the plane increases, the aerodynamic drag increases in proportion to the square of the airspeed. Eventually, the aircraft reaches a new cruise speed where the thrust from the UDF engines is just offset by the drag. The equations used to estimate the velocity and acceleration of the aircraft from the time that the throttle is reset until the plane reaches its new cruise speed (at approximately 120 s) are the following:

$$\text{velocity} = 0.00001 \text{ time}^3 - 0.00488 \text{ time}^2 + 0.75795 \text{ time} + 181.3566$$
$$\text{acceleration} = 3 - 0.000062 \text{ velocity}^2$$

Plots of these functions are shown in Figure 2.2. Note that the acceleration approaches zero as the velocity approaches its new cruise speed.

Write a program that asks the user to enter a time value that represents the time elapsed (in seconds) since the power level was increased. Compute and print the corresponding acceleration and velocity of the aircraft at the new time value.

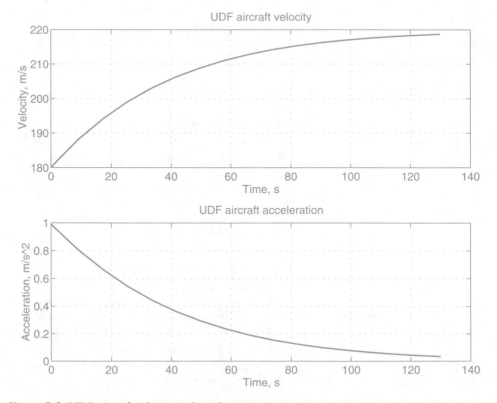

Figure 2.2 *UDF aircraft velocity and acceleration.*

1.   **PROBLEM STATEMENT**

Compute the new velocity and acceleration of the aircraft after a change in power level.

2.   **INPUT/OUTPUT DESCRIPTION**

The following diagram shows that the input to the program is a time value and that the output of the program is the pair of new velocity and acceleration values.

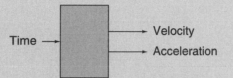

3.   **HAND EXAMPLE**

Suppose that the new time value is 50 seconds. Using the equations given for the velocity and accelerations, we can compute these values:

velocity = 208.3 m/s

acceleration = 0.31 m/s^2

4.   **ALGORITHM DEVELOPMENT**

The first step in the development of an algorithm is the decomposition of the problem solution into a set of sequentially executed steps:

Decomposition Outline:

   1. *Read new time value.*
   2. *Compute corresponding velocity and acceleration values.*
   3. *Print new velocity and acceleration.*

Because this program is a very simple program, we can convert the decomposition directly to C.

```
/*------------------------------------------------------*/
/*  Program chapter2_1                                  */
/*                                                      */
```

```
/*  This program estimates new velocity and        */
/*  acceleration values for a specified time.       */

#include <stdio.h>
#include <stdlib.h>
#include <math.h>

main()
{
   /*  Declare variables.  */
   double time, velocity, acceleration;

   /*  Get time value from the keyboard.  */
   printf("Enter new time value in seconds: ");
   scanf("%lf",&time);

   /*  Compute velocity and acceleration.  */
   velocity = 0.00001*pow(time,3) - 0.00488*pow(time,2)
            + 0.75795*time + 181.3566;
   acceleration = 3 - 0.000062*velocity*velocity;

   /*  Print velocity and acceleration.  */
   printf("Velocity = %8.3f m/s \n",velocity);
   printf("Acceleration = %8.3f m/s^2 \n",acceleration);

   /*  Exit program.  */
   return EXIT_SUCCESS;
}
/*-----------------------------------------------------*/
```

5. TESTING

We first test the program using the data from the hand example. This generates the following interaction:

```
Enter new time value in seconds: 50
Velocity =  208.304 m/s
Acceleration =    0.310 m/s^2
```

Because the values computed match the hand example, we can then test the program with other time values. If the values had not matched the hand example, we would need to determine if the error is in the hand example or in the program.

SUMMARY

In this chapter, we presented the C statements necessary to write simple programs that compute and print new values. We also presented the statement that allows us to enter information through the keyboard when the program is executing. The computations that were presented included the standard arithmetic operations plus a large number of functions that can be used to perform the types of computations needed for engineering solutions.

KEY TERMS

abbreviated assignment
address operator
argument
assignment statement
associativity
binary operator
case sensitive
cast operator
comment
composition
constant
control string
conversion specifier
declaration
escape character
exponential notation
expression
field width
floating-point value
garbage value
identifier
keyword
mantissa

memory snapshot
modulus
multiple assignment
overflow
parameter
postfix
precedence
precision
prefix
preprocessor directive
prompt
range
scientific notation
Standard C library
statement
symbolic constant
system dependent
truncate
type specifier
unary operator
underflow
variable

C STATEMENT SUMMARY

Preprocessor directives to include information from the files in the Standard C library:

```
#include <stdio.h>
#include <stdlib.h>
#include <math.h>
```

Preprocessor directive to define a symbolic constant

```
#define PI 3.141593
```

Declarations for integers

```
short sum=0;
int year_1, year_2;
long k;
```

Declarations for floating-point values

```
float height_1, height_2;
double length=10, side1, side2;
long double distance, velocity;
```

Assignment statement

```
area = 0.5*base*(height_1 + height_2);
```

Keyboard input statement

```
scanf("%i",&year);
```

Screen output statement

```
printf("The area is %f square feet \n",area);
```

Program exit statement

```
return EXIT_SUCCESS;
```

Style NOTES

1.   Use comments throughout a program to improve the readability and to document the steps in it.
2.   Use blank lines and indenting to identify the structure of a program.
3.   Use the units in a variable name when possible.
4.   Use symbolic constants for engineering constants such as π; they should be uppercase so that they are easily identified.
5.   Use consistent spacing around arithmetic and assignment operators.
6.   Use parentheses in complicated expressions to improve readability.

7. The evaluation of long expressions should be broken into several statements.
8. Be sure to include units along with numerical values in the output of a program.
9. Use a prompt to the user to describe the information and units for values to be entered from the keyboard.

DEBUGGING NOTES

1. Declarations and C statements must end with a semicolon.
2. Preprocessor directives do not end with a semicolon.
3. If possible, avoid assignments that could potentially cause information to be lost.
4. Use parentheses in a long expression to be sure that it is evaluated as desired.
5. Use double precision or extended precision to avoid problems with exponent overflow or underflow.
6. Be sure that the specifier matches the variable type in a **scanf** statement.
7. Errors can occur if user input values cannot be converted correctly to the specifier variable type in a **scanf** statement.
8. Do not forget the address operator with identifiers in the **scanf** statement.
9. Remember that symbolic constant definitions do not end with a semicolon.
10. In nested function references, each set of arguments must be in its own set of parentheses.
11. Remember that the logarithmic functions cannot be used with negative or zero values for arguments.
12. Be sure to use angles in radians with the trigonometric functions.
13. Remember that many of the inverse trigonometric functions and hyperbolic functions have restrictions on the ranges of allowable input values.

PROBLEMS

Conversions. This set of problems involves conversions of a value in one unit to another unit. Each program should prompt the user for a value in the specified units and then print the converted value, along with the new units.

1. Write a program to convert miles to kilometers. (Recall that 1 mi = 1.6093440 km.)
2. Write a program to convert pounds to kilograms. (Recall that 1 kg = 2.205 lb.)
3. Write a program that converts degrees Fahrenheit (T_F) to degrees Rankin (T_R). (Recall that $T_F = T_R - 459.67°R$.)

Areas and Volumes. These problems involve computing an area or a volume using input from the user. Each program should include a prompt to the user to enter the variables needed.

4.   Write a program to compute the area of a triangle with base b and height h. (Recall that $A = \frac{1}{2} b \cdot h$.)

5.   Write a program to compute the area of a sector of a circle when d is the angle in degrees between the radii. (Recall that $A = r^2\theta/2$, where θ is the angle in radians.)

6.   Write a program to compute the volume of a sphere of radius r. (Recall that $V = 4/3\pi r^3$.)

Amino Acid Molecular Weights. The amino acids in proteins are composed of atoms of oxygen, carbon, nitrogen, sulfur, and hydrogen, as shown in Table 2.7. The molecular weights of the individual elements are

Element	Atomic Weight
oxygen	15.9994
carbon	12.011
nitrogen	14.00674
sulfur	32.066
hydrogen	1.00794

TABLE 2.7 Amino Acid Molecules

Amino Acid	O	C	N	S	H
Alanine	2	3	1	0	7
Arginine	2	6	4	0	15
Asparagine	3	4	2	0	8
Aspartic	4	4	1	0	6
Cysteine	2	3	1	1	7
Glutamic	4	5	1	0	8
Glutamine	3	5	2	0	10
Glycine	2	2	1	0	5
Histidine	2	6	3	0	10
Isoleucine	2	6	1	0	13
Leucine	2	6	1	0	13
Lysine	2	6	2	0	15
Methionine	2	5	1	1	11
Phenylanlanine	2	9	1	0	11
Proline	2	5	1	0	10
Serine	3	3	1	0	7
Threonine	3	4	1	0	9
Tryptophan	2	11	2	0	11
Tyrosine	3	9	1	0	11
Valine	2	5	1	0	11

7. Write a program that asks the user to enter the number of atoms of each of the five elements for an amino acid. Then compute and print the molecular weight for this amino acid.

8. Write a program that asks the user to enter the number of atoms of each of the five elements for an amino acid. Then compute and print the average weight of the atoms in the amino acid.

Logarithms to the Base b. To compute the logarithm of x to base b, we can use the following relationship:

$$\log_b x = \frac{\log_e x}{\log_e b}$$

9. Write a program that reads a positive number and then computes and prints the logarithm of the value to base 2. For example, the logarithm of 8 to the base 2 is 3, because $2^3 = 8$.

10. Write a program that reads a positive number and then computes and prints the logarithm of the value to the base 8. For example, the logarithm of 64 to the base 8 is 2, because $8^2 = 64$.

3

Courtesy of National Center for Atmospheric Research/
University Corporation for Atmospheric Research/
National Science Foundation.

GRAND CHALLENGE:
Global Change

Weather balloons are used to collect data from the upper atmosphere. The balloons
are filled with helium and rise to an equilibrium point where the difference between
the densities of the helium inside the balloon and the air outside the balloon is just
enough to support the weight of the balloon. During the day, the sun warms the
balloon, causing it to rise to a new equilibrium point; in the evening, the balloon
cools, and it descends to a lower altitude. The balloon can be used to measure the
temperature, pressure, humidity, chemical concentrations, or other properties of
the air around the balloon. A weather balloon may stay aloft for only a few hours
or as long as several years collecting environmental data. The balloon falls back
to earth as the helium leaks out or is released.

Control Structures and Data Files

OBJECTIVES

In this chapter we present structured programming in terms of sequence, selection, and repetition structures. After defining these structures using pseudocode and flowcharts, we discuss the C statements for implementing these structures. Sequence structures do not require new statements. The selection structure requires conditional expressions and `if` statements in order to provide alternative paths in a program. The repetition structure is implemented with three different loop structures—`while` loops, `do/while` loops, and `for` loops. An example that applies to weather balloons is used to illustrate conditional statements and loops. We also introduce simple data files at this point because they are commonly used in solving engineering problems.

3.1   Algorithm Development

In Chapter 2, the C programs that we developed were very simple. The steps were sequential and typically involved reading information from the keyboard, computing new information, and then printing the new information. In solving engineering problems, most of the solutions require more complicated steps; thus, we need to expand the algorithm development part of our problem-solving process.

TOP-DOWN DESIGN

Top-down design presents a "big picture" description of the problem solution in sequential steps. This overall description of the problem is refined until the steps are detailed enough to translate to language statements.

Decomposition Outline. We used **decomposition outlines** in Chapters 1 and 2 to provide the first definition of a problem solution. This outline is written in sequential steps and can be shown in a diagram or a step-by-step outline. For very simple problems, such as the one below that was developed in Chapter 2, we can go from the decomposition outline directly to the C statements:

Decomposition Outline:
1. *Read new time value.*
2. *Compute corresponding velocity and acceleration values.*
3. *Print new velocity and acceleration.*

However, for most problem solutions, we need to refine the decomposition outline into a description with more detail. This process is often referred to as a **divide-and-conquer** strategy, because we keep breaking the problem solution into smaller and smaller portions. To describe this **stepwise refinement**, we use pseudocode or flowcharts.

Stepwise refinement

Refinement with Pseudocode and Flowcharts. The refinement of an outline into more detailed steps can be done with pseudocode or a flowchart. **Pseudocode** uses English-like statements to describe the steps in an algorithm; a **flowchart** uses a diagram to describe the steps in an algorithm. The fundamental steps in most algorithms are shown in Figure 3.1, along with the corresponding notation in pseudocode and flowcharts.

Pseudocode and flowcharts are tools to help us determine the order of steps to solve a problem. Both tools are commonly used, although generally not with the same problem. Sometimes we need to go through several levels of pseudocode or flowcharts to develop complex problem solutions; this is the stepwise refinement that we mentioned previously in this section. Decomposition outlines, pseudocode, and flowcharts are working models of the solution and are not unique. Each person working on a solution will have different decomposition outlines and pseudocode or flowchart descriptions, just as the C programs developed by different people will be somewhat different, although they solve the same problem.

Basic Operation	Pseudocode Notation	Flowchart Symbol

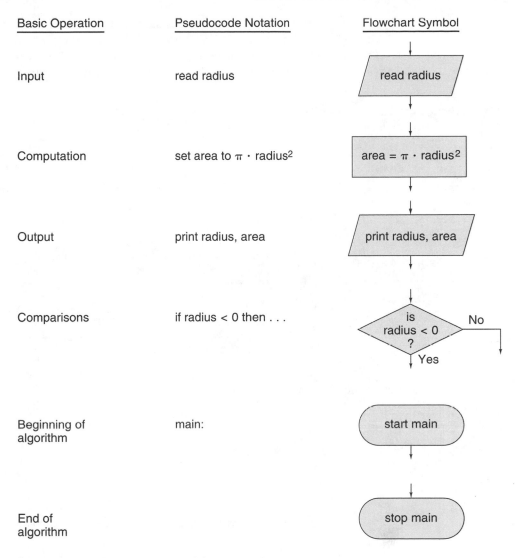

Input	read radius	
Computation	set area to $\pi \cdot radius^2$	
Output	print radius, area	
Comparisons	if radius < 0 then . . .	
Beginning of algorithm	main:	
End of algorithm		

Figure 3.1 *Pseudocode notation and flowchart symbols.*

STRUCTURED PROGRAMMING

A **structured program** is one written using simple control structures to organize the solution to a problem. A simple structure is usually defined to be a sequence, a selection, or a repetition. A **sequence** structure contains steps that are performed one after another; a **selection** structure contains one set of steps that is performed if a condition is true and another set of steps that is performed if the condition is false; a **repetition** structure contains a set of steps that is repeated as long as a condition is true. We now discuss each of these simple structures and use pseudocode and flowcharts to give specific examples.

Sequence. A sequence contains steps that are performed one after another. All the programs presented in Chapters 1 and 2 have a sequence structure. For example, the flowchart for the program that computed the velocity and acceleration of the aircraft with the unducted engine is shown in Figure 3.2.

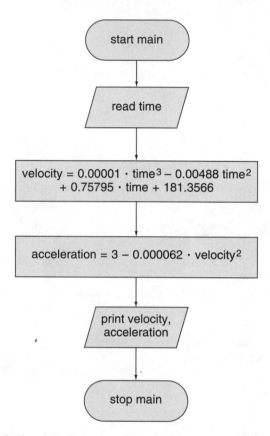

Figure 3.2. *Flowchart for unducted fan problem solution from Section 2.6.*

Condition

Selection. A selection structure contains a **condition** that can be evaluated as either true or false. If the condition is true, one set of statements is executed; if the condition is false, another set of statements is executed. For example, suppose that we have computed values for the numerator and denominator of a fraction. Before we compute the division, we want to be sure that the denominator is not close to zero. Therefore, the condition that we want to test is "denominator close to zero." If the condition is true, we want to print a message indicating that we cannot compute the value. If the condition is false, which means that the denominator is not close to zero, then we compute and print the value of the fraction. In defining this condition, we need to define "close to zero." For this example, we will assume that close to zero means that the absolute value is less than 0.0001. A pseudocode description is on the next page, and a flowchart description of this structure is shown in Figure 3.3.

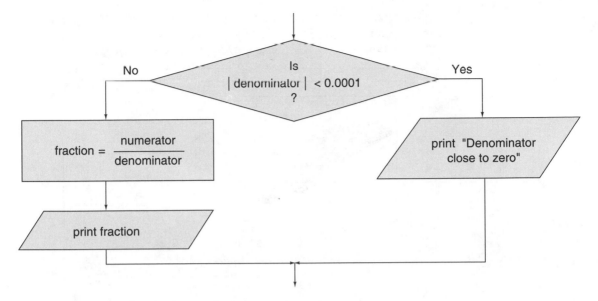

Figure 3.3 *Flowchart for selection structure.*

> *if* | *denominator*| < 0.0001
> > *print "Denominator close to zero"*
>
> *else*
> > *set fraction to numerator/denominator*
> > *print fraction*

Note that this structure also contains a sequence structure (compute a fraction and then print the fraction) that is executed when the condition is false. We give more variations of the selection structure later in this chapter.

Repetition. The repetition structure allows us to repeat a set of steps as long as a condition is true. For example, we might want to compute a set of velocity values that correspond to time values of 0, 1, 2, . . . , 10 seconds. We do not want to develop a sequential structure that has a statement to compute the velocity for a time of 0, another statement to compute the velocity for a time of 1, and then another statement to compute the velocity for a time of 2, and so on. Although this structure would require only 11 statements in this case, it could require hundreds of statements if we wanted to compute the velocity values over a long period of time. If we use the repetition structure, we can develop a solution in which we initialize the time to 0. Then, as long as the time value is less than or equal to 10, we compute and print a velocity value and increment the time value by 1. When the time value is greater than 10, we exit the structure. Figure 3.4 contains the flowchart for this repetition structure; the pseudocode follows:

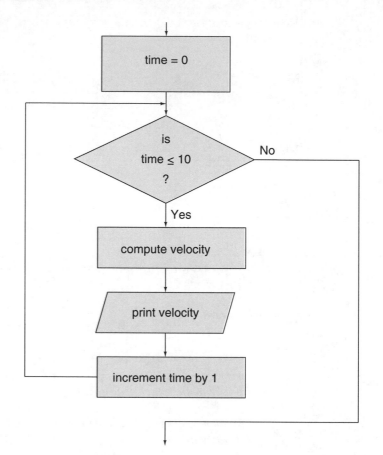

Figure 3.4 *Flowchart for repetition structure.*

set time to 0
while time ≤ 10
    compute velocity
    print velocity
    increment time by 1

3.2   Conditional Expressions

Because both selection and repetition structures use conditions, we must discuss conditions before presenting the statements that implement selection and repetition structures. A **condition** is an expression that can be evaluated to be true or false and is composed of expressions combined with relational operators; a condition can also include logical operators. In this section we present relational operators and logical operators and discuss the evaluation order when they are combined in a single condition.

RELATIONAL OPERATORS

The **relational operators** that can be used to compare two expressions in C are shown in the following list:

Relational Operator	Interpretation
<	is less than
<=	is less than or equal to
>	is greater than
>=	is greater than or equal to
==	is equal to
!=	is not equal to

Blanks can be used on either side of a relational operator, but blanks cannot be used to separate a two-character operator such as ==.

Example conditions are the following:

```
a < b
x+y >= 10.5
fabs(denominator) < 0.0001
```

Given the values of the identifiers in these conditions, we can evaluate each one to be true or false. For example, if **a** is equal to 5 and **b** is equal to 8.4, then **a < b** is a true condition. If **x** is equal to 2.3 and **y** is equal to 4.1, then **x+y >= 10.5** is a false condition. If **denominator** is equal to -0.0025, then **fabs(denominator) < 0.0001** is a false condition. *Note that we use spaces around the relational operator in a logical expression, but not around the arithmetic operators in the conditions.*

Style

In C, a true condition is assigned a value of 1; a false condition is assigned a value of zero. Therefore, the following statement is valid:

```
d = b>c;
```

If **b>c**, the value of **d** is 1; otherwise, the value of **d** is zero. Because a condition is given a value, it is valid to use a value in place of a condition. For example, consider the following statement:

```
if (a)
    count++;
```

If the condition value is zero, the condition is assumed to be false; if the value is nonzero, the condition is assumed to be true. Therefore, in the statement above, the value of **count** will be incremented if **a** is nonzero.

LOGICAL OPERATORS

Logical operators can also be used within conditions. However, logical operators compare conditions, not expressions. C supports three logical operators: not, and, or. These logical operators are represented by the following symbols:

Logical Operator	Symbol
not	!
and	&&
or	||

For example, consider the following condition:

```
a<b && b<c
```

Style

The relational operators have higher precedence than the logical operator; therefore, this condition is read "**a** is less than **b**, and **b** is less than **c**." *In order to make a logical statement more readable, we insert spaces around the logical operator, but not around the relational operators.* Given values for **a**, **b**, and **c**, we can evaluate this condition as true or false. For example, if **a** is equal to 1, **b** is equal to 5, and **c** is equal to 8, the condition is true. If **a** is equal to −2, **b** is equal to 9, and **c** is equal to 2, the condition is false.

If **A** and **B** are conditions, the logical operators can be used to generate new conditions **A && B, A || B, !A**, and **!B**. The condition **A && B** is true only if both **A** and **B** are true. The condition **A || B** is true if either or both **A** and **B** are true. The **!** operator changes the value of the condition with which it is used. Thus, the condition **!A** is true only if **A** is false, and the condition **!B** is true only if **B** is false. These definitions are summarized in Table 3.1.

When expressions with logical operators are executed, C will evaluate only as much of the expression as necessary to evaluate it. For example, if **A** is false, then the expression **A && B** is also false, and there is no need to evaluate **B**. Similarly, if **A** is true, then the expression **A || B** is true, and there is no need to evaluate **B**.

PRECEDENCE AND ASSOCIATIVITY

A condition can contain several logical operators as in the following:

```
!(b==c || b==5.5)
```

The hierarchy, from highest to lowest, is **!, &&, ||**, but parentheses can be used to change the hierarchy. In this example, the expressions **b==c** and **b==5.5** are evaluated first. Suppose **b** is equal to 3 and **c** is equal to 5. Then neither expression is true, so the expression **b==c || b==5.5** is false. We then apply the **!** operator to the false condition, which gives a true condition. Blanks cannot be used to separate the characters in either **||** or **&&**. A common error is to use = instead of == in a logical expression.

TABLE 3.1 Logical Operators

A	B	A && B	A || B	!A	!B
False	False	False	False	True	True
False	True	False	True	True	False
True	False	False	True	False	True
True	True	True	True	False	False

A condition can contain both arithmetic operators and relational operators, as well as logical operators. Table 3.2 contains the precedence and the associativity order for the elements in a condition.

TABLE 3.2 Operator Precedence for Arithmetic, Relational, and Logical Operators

Precedence	Operation	Associativity
1	( )	innermost first
2	+ - ++ -- (type) !	right to left (unary)
3	* / %	left to right
4	+ -	left to right
5	< <= > >=	left to right
6	== !=	left to right
7	&&	left to right
8	||	left to right
9	= += -= *= /= %=	right to left

Practice!

Determine if the following conditions are true or false. Assume that the following variables have been declared and given these values:

(handwritten: 1, 5 / 3 / 4.5)

a $\boxed{5.5}$ b $\boxed{1.5}$ k $\boxed{3}$

1. a < 10.0+k   *True*
2. a+b >= 6.5   *True*
3. !(a == 3*b)   *True*

4. -k <= k+6   *True*
5. a<10 && a>5   *True*
6. fabs(k)>3 || k<b-a   *False*

3.3   Selection Statements

The **if** statement allows us to test a condition and then perform statements based on whether the condition is true or false. C contains two forms of **if** statements—the simple **if** statement and the **if/else** statement.

SIMPLE if STATEMENT

The simplest form of an **if** statement has the following general form:

```
if (condition)
    statement 1;
```

Style

If the condition is true, we execute statement 1; if the condition is false, we skip statement 1. *The statement within the* if *statement is indented so that it is easier to visualize the structure of the program from the statements.*

Compound statement

If we wish to execute several statements (or a sequence structure) if the condition is true, we use a **compound statement**, or **block**, which is composed of a set of statements enclosed in braces. The location of the braces is a matter of style; two common styles are shown:

```
Style 1                        Style 2
if (condition)                 if (condition) {
{                                  statement 1;
    statement 1;                   statement 2;
    statement 2;                   . . .
    . . .                          statement n;
    statement n;               }
}
```

In the text solutions, we use the first style convention; thus, both braces are on lines by themselves. Although this makes the program a little longer, it also makes it easier to notice if a brace has been mistakenly omitted. Figure 3.5 contains flowcharts of the control flow with simple if statements containing either one statement to execute or several statements to execute if the condition is true.

A specific example of an **if** statement follows:

```
if (a < 50)
{
    ++count;
    sum += a;
}
```

If **a** is less than 50, then **count** is incremented by 1, and **a** is added to **sum**; otherwise, these two statements are skipped.

Note that **if** statements can also be nested; the following example includes an **if** statement within an **if** statement:

```
if (a < 50)
{
    ++count;
    sum += a;
    if (b > a)
        b = 0;
}
```

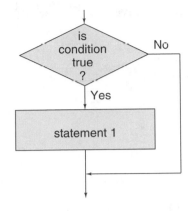

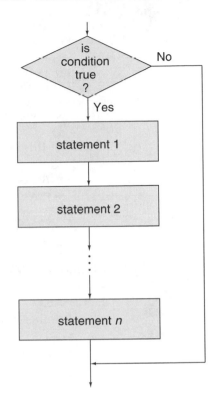

Figure 3.5 *Flowcharts for selection statements.*

If **a** is less than 50, we increment **count** by 1 and add **a** to **sum**. In addition, if **b** is greater than **a**, then we also set **b** to zero. If **a** is not less than 50, then we skip all these statements. *Be sure to indent the statements in each if statement when they are nested.*

Style

if/else STATEMENT

An **if/else** statement allows us to execute one set of statements if a condition is true and a different set if the condition is false. The simplest form of an **if/else** statement is the following:

```
if (condition)
    statement 1;
else
    statement 2;
```

Empty statement

Statements 1 and 2 can also be replaced by compound statements. Statement 1 or statement 2 can also be an **empty statement**, which is a semicolon. If statement 2 is an empty statement, the **if/else** statement should probably be posed as a simple **if** statement. There are situations in which it is convenient to use an empty statement for statement 1; however, these statements can also be rewritten as a simple **if** statement with the condition reversed. For example, the following two statements are equivalent:

```
if (a < b)          if (a >= b)
   ;                   count++;
else
   count++;
```

Consider this **if/else** statement:

```
if (d <= 30)
   velocity = 0.425 + 0.00175*d*d;
else
   velocity = 0.625 + 0.12*d - 0.0025*d*d;
```

In this example, **velocity** is computed with the first assignment statement if the distance **d** is less than or equal to 30; otherwise, **velocity** is computed with the second assignment statement. A flowchart for this **if/else** statement is shown in Figure 3.6.

Another example of the **if/else** statement is the following:

```
if (fabs(denominator) < 0.0001)
   printf("Denominator of x is equal to zero");
else
{
   fraction = numerator/denominator;
   printf("fraction = %f \n",fraction);
}
```

In this example, we examine the absolute value of the variable **denominator**. If this value is close to zero, we print a message indicating that we cannot perform

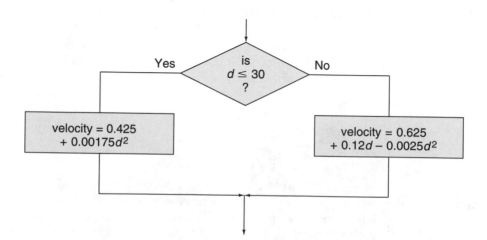

Figure 3.6 *Flowchart for selection structure.*

the division. If the value of **denominator** is not close to zero, we compute and print the value of **x**. The flowchart for this statement was shown in Figure 3.3.

Consider the following set of nested **if/else** statements:

```
if (x > y)
    if (y < z)
        k++;
    else
        m++;
else
    j++;
```

The value of **k** is incremented when **x > y** and **y < z**. The value of **m** is incremented when **x > y** and **y >= z**. The value of **j** is incremented when **x <= y**. With careful indenting, this statement is straightforward to follow. Suppose that we now eliminate the **else** portion of the inner **if** statement. If we keep the same indention, the statements become the following:

```
if (x > y)
    if (y < z)
        k++;
else
    j++;
```

It might appear that **j** is incremented when **x <= y**, but that is not correct. The C compiler will associate an **else** statement with the closest **if** statement within a block. Therefore, no matter what indenting is used, the statement above is executed as if it were the following:

```
if (x > y)
    if (y < z)
        k++;
    else
        j++;
```

Thus, **j** is incremented when **x > y** and **y >= z**. If we intend for **j** to be incremented when **x <= y**, then we must use braces to define the inner statement as a block:

```
if (x > y)
{
    if (y < z)
        k++;
}
else
    j++;
```

Style

To avoid confusion and possible errors when using nested if/else *statements, you should routinely use braces to clearly define the blocks of statements that go together.*

In this section, we have presented a number of ways to compare values in selection statements. A caution is necessary when comparing floating-point values. For example, in an example in this section, we did not compare **denominator** to zero, but instead used a condition to see if the absolute value of **denominator** were less than a small value. Similarly, if we wanted to know if **y** was close to the value 10.5, we should use a condition such as **fabs(y-10.5) < = 0.0001** instead of **y == 10.5**. In general, do not use the equality operator with floating-point values.

Practice!

In problems 1 through 6, give the corresponding C statements. Assume that the variables have been declared and have reasonable values.

1. If **time** is greater than 15.0, increment **time** by 1.0.
2. When the square root of **poly** is less than 0.5, print the value of **poly**.
3. If the difference between **volt_1** and **volt_2** is larger than 10.0, print the values of **volt_1** and **volt_2**.
4. If the natural logarithm of **x** is greater than or equal to 3, set **time** equal to zero and decrement **count**.
5. If **dist** is less than 50.0 and **time** is greater than 10.0, increment **time** by 2; otherwise, increment **time** by 2.5.
6. If **dist** is greater than or equal to 100.0, increment **time** by 2.0. If **dist** is between 50 and 100, increment **time** by 1. Otherwise, increment **time** by 0.5.

3.4   Loop Structures

Loops

Loops are used to implement repetitive structures. C contains three different loop structures—the **while** loop, the **do/while** loop, and the **for** loop. In addition, C allows us to use loops two additional statements with loops to modify their performance—the **break** statement and the **continue** statement.

Before presenting these loop structures, we would like to present two debugging suggestions that are useful when trying to find errors in programs that contain loops. When compiling longer programs, it is not uncommon to have a large number of compiler errors. Rather than trying to find each error separately, we suggest that you recompile your program after correcting several obvious syntax errors. One error will often generate several error messages. Some of these error messages may describe errors that are not in your program, but were printed because the original error confused the compiler.

The second debugging suggestion relates to errors inside a loop. When you want to determine if the steps in a loop are working the way that you want, include **printf** statements in the loop to provide a memory snapshot of key variables each time the loop is executed. Then, if there is an error, you have much of the information that you need to determine what is causing the error.

while LOOP

The general form of a **while** loop is shown below:

```
while (condition)
    statement;
```

The condition is evaluated before the statement within the loop is executed. (The statement may also be a compound statement.) If the condition is false, the loop statement is skipped, and execution continues with the statement following the **while** loop. If the condition is true, the loop statement is executed, and the condition is evaluated again. If it is still true, then the statement is executed again, and the condition is evaluated again. This repetition continues until the condition is false. The statement within the loop must modify variables that are used in the condition; otherwise, the value of the condition will never change, and we will either never execute the statements in the loop or we will never be able to exit the loop. An **infinite loop** is generated if the condition in a **while** loop is always true. Most systems have a system-defined limit on the amount of time that can be used by a program and will generate an execution error when this limit is exceeded. Other systems require that the user enter a special set of characters, such as the control key followed by the character c (abbreviated as ^c) to stop or **abort** the execution of a program. Nearly everyone eventually writes a program that inadvertently contains an infinite loop, so be sure you know the special characters to abort the execution of a program for your system.

Infinite loop

The following pseudocode and program use a **while** loop to generate a conversion table for converting degrees to radians. The degree values start at $0°$, increment by $10°$, and go through $360°$.

Refinement in Pseudocode
main: set degrees to zero
         while degrees ≤ 360
              convert degrees to radians
              print degrees, radians
              add 10 to degrees

```
/*------------------------------------------------------*/
/*  Program chapter3_1                          */
/*                                              */
/*  This program prints a degree-to-radian table    */
/*  using a while loop structure.               */

#include <stdio.h>
#include <stdlib.h>
#define PI 3.141593
```

```
main()
{
   /*   Declare and initialize variables.   */
   int degrees=0;
   double radians;

   /*   Print radians and degrees in a loop.   */
   printf("Degrees to Radians \n");
   while (degrees <= 360)
   {
      radians = degrees*PI/180;
      printf("%6i %9.6f \n",degrees,radians);
      degrees += 10;
   }

   /*   Exit program.   */
   return EXIT_SUCCESS;
}
/*------------------------------------------------------*/
```

The first few lines of output from the program follow:

```
Degrees to Radians
     0   0.000000
    10   0.174533
    20   0.349066
   . . .
```

do/while LOOP

The do/while loop is similar to the while loop except that the condition is tested at the end of the loop instead of at the beginning of the loop. Testing the condition at the end of the loop ensures that the do/while loop is always executed at least once; a while loop may not be executed at all if the condition is initially false. The general form of the do/while loop is

```
do
    statement;
while (condition);
```

The following pseudocode and program print the degree-to conversion table using a do/while loop instead of a while loop:

Refinement in Pseudocode:

main: *set degrees to zero*
           do
                   convert degrees to radians
                   print degrees, radians
                   add 10 to degrees
           while degrees ≤ 360

```
/*--------------------------------------------------------*/
/*  Program chapter3_2                                    */
/*                                                        */
/*  This program prints a degree-to-radian table         */
/*  using a do-while loop structure.                      */

#include <stdio.h>
#include <stdlib.h>
#define PI 3.141593

main()
{
   /*  Declare and initialize variables.  */
   int degrees=0;
   double radians;

   /*  Print degrees and radians in a loop.  */
   printf("Degrees to Radians \n");
   do
   {
      radians = degrees*PI/180;
      printf("%6i %9.6f \n",degrees,radians);
      degrees += 10;
   } while (degrees <= 360);

   /*  Exit program.  */
   return EXIT_SUCCESS;
}
/*--------------------------------------------------------*/
```

for LOOP

Many programs require loops that are based on the value of a variable that increments (or decrements) by the same amount each time through the loop. When the variable reaches a specified value, we want to exit the loop. This type of loop can be implemented as a **while** loop, but it can also be easily implemented with the **for** loop. The general form of the **for** loop is

```
for (expression_1; expression_2; expression_3)
   statement;
```

Loop-control variable

Expression_1 is used to initialize the **loop-control variable**, expression_2 specifies the condition that should be true to continue the loop repetition, and expression_3 specifies the modification to the loop-control variable.

For example, if we want to execute a loop 10 times, with the value of the variable **k** going from 1 to 10 in increments of 1, we could use the following:

```
for (k=1; k<=10; k++)
   statement;
```

If we want to execute a loop with the value of the variable **n** going from 20 to 0 in increments of −2, we could use this loop structure:

```
for (n=20; n>=0; n=n-2)
    statement;
```

The **for** loop could also have been written in this form:

```
for (n=20; n>=0; n-=2)
    statement;
```

Both forms are valid, but the abbreviated form is commonly used because it is shorter.

The following expression computes the number of times that a **for** loop will be executed:

$$\text{floor}\left(\frac{\text{final value} - \text{initial value}}{\text{increment}}\right) + 1$$

If this value is negative, the loop is not executed. Thus, if a **for** statement has the following structure:

```
for (k=5; k<=83; k+=4)
    statement;
```

it would be executed the following number of times:

$$\text{floor}\left(\frac{83 - 5}{4}\right) + 1 = \text{floor}\left(\frac{78}{4}\right) + 1 = 20$$

The value of **k** would be 5, then 9, then 13, and so on, until the final value of 81. The loop would not be executed with the value of 85 because the loop condition is not true when **k** is equal to 85.

The following pseudocode and program print the degree-to-radian conversion table shown earlier with a **while** loop, now modified to use a **for** loop. Note that the pseudocode for the **while** loop solution to this problem and the pseudocode for the **do** loop solution to this problem are identical.

Refinement in Pseudocode:

main: *set degrees to zero*
            while degrees ≤ 360
                convert degrees to radians
                print degrees, radians
                add 10 to degrees

```
/*-----------------------------------------------------*/
/*   Program chapter3_3                                 */
/*                                                      */
/*   This program prints a degree-to-radian table       */
/*   using a for loop structure.                        */

#include <stdio.h>
#include <stdlib.h>
#define PI 3.141593

main()
{
   /*  Declare the variables.  */
   int degrees;
   double radians;

   /*  Print degrees and radians in a loop.  */
   printf("Degrees to Radians \n");
   for (degrees=0; degrees<=360; degrees+=10)
   {
     radians = degrees*PI/180;
     printf("%6i %9.6f \n",degrees,radians);
   }

   /*  Exit program.  */
   return EXIT_SUCCESS;
}
/*-----------------------------------------------------*/
```

Note that the value of **degrees** did not need to be initialized in the declaration because it is initialized in the **for** loop statement.

Practice!

Determine the number of times that the **for** loops below are executed.

1. `for (k=3; k<=20; k++)` $\left(\frac{20-3}{1}\right)+1$ $\frac{17}{1}+1=18$
   `statement;`

2. `for (k=3; k<=20; ++k)` $\left(\frac{20-3}{1}\right)+1$ $\frac{17}{1}+1=18$
   `statement;`

3. `for (count=-2; count<=14; count++)` $\left(\frac{14--2}{1}\right)+1$ $\frac{16}{1}+1=17$
   `statement;`

4. `for (k=-2; k>=-10; k--)` $\left(\frac{-10--2}{+1}\right)+1 = \frac{-10}{+1} = 13$ $-10+1=-9$
   `statement;`

5. `for (time=10; time>=0; time--)`   infinite loop
   `statement;`

6. `for (time=10; time>=5; time++)` $\left(\frac{5-10}{1}\right)+5$ 11
   `statement;`

break AND continue STATEMENTS

The **break** statement can be used with any of the loop structures presented in this section to immediately exit from the loop in which it is contained. In contrast, the **continue** statement is used to skip the remaining statements in the current pass or **iteration** of the loop and then continue with the next iteration of the loop. Thus, in a **while** loop or a **do/while** loop, the condition is evaluated after the **continue** statement is executed to determine if the statements in the loop are to be executed again. In a **for** loop, the loop-control variable is modified, and the condition is evaluated to determine if the statements in the loop are to be executed again. Both the **break** and **continue** statements are useful in exiting either the current iteration or the entire loop when error conditions are encountered.

Interation

To illustrate the difference between the **break** and the **continue** statements, consider the following loop that reads values from the keyboard:

```
sum = 0;
for (k=1; k<=20; k++)
{
    scanf("%lf",&x);
    if (x > 10.0)
       break;
    sum += x;
}
printf("Sum = %f \n",sum);
```

This loop reads up to 20 values from the keyboard. If all 20 values are less than or equal to 10.0, the statements compute the sum of the values and print the sum. But, if a value is read that is greater than 10.0, the **break** statement causes control to break out of the loop and execute the **printf** statement. Thus, the sum printed is only the sum of the values up to the value greater than 10.0.

Now, consider this variation of the previous loop:

```
sum = 0;
for (k=1; k<=20; k++)
{
    scanf("%lf",&x);
    if (x > 10.0)
       continue;
    sum += x;
}
printf("Sum = %f \n",sum);
```

In this loop, the sum of all 20 values is printed if all values are less than or equal to 10.0. However, if a value is greater than 10.0, the **continue** statement causes control to skip the rest of the statements in that iteration of the loop and to continue with the next iteration of the loop. Hence, the sum printed is the sum of all values in the 20 values that are less than or equal to 10.

3.5   Problem Solving Applied: Weather Balloons

Weather balloons are used to gather temperature and pressure data at various altitudes in the atmosphere. The balloon rises because the density of the helium in the balloon is less than the density of the surrounding air outside the balloon. As the balloon rises, the surrounding air becomes less dense; thus, the balloon's ascent slows until it reaches a point of equilibrium. During the day, sunlight warms the helium trapped inside the balloon, which causes the helium to expand and become less dense and the balloon to rise higher. During the night, however, the helium in the balloon cools and becomes more dense, causing the balloon to descend to a lower altitude. The next day, the sun heats the helium again and the balloon rises. Over time this process generates a set of altitude measurements that can be approximated with a polynomial equation.

Assume that the following polynomial represents the altitude or height in meters during the first 48 hours following the launch of a weather balloon:

$$alt(t) = -0.12t^4 + 12t^3 - 380t^2 + 4100t + 220$$

where the units of t are hours. The corresponding polynomial model for the velocity in meters per hour of the weather balloon is as follows:

$$v(t) = -0.48t^3 + 36t^2 - 760t + 4100$$

Print a table of the altitude and the velocity for this weather balloon using units of meters and meters/second. Let the user enter the start time, increment in time between lines of the table, and ending time, where all the time values must be less than 48 hours. In addition to printing the table, also print the peak altitude from the table and its corresponding time.

1.   **PROBLEM STATEMENT**

Using the polynomials that represent the altitude and velocity for a weather balloon, print a table using units of meters and meters/second. Also find the maximum altitude (or height) and its corresponding time.

2.   **INPUT/OUTPUT DESCRIPTION**

The following I/O diagram shows the user input that represents the starting time, time increment, and ending time for the table. The output is the table of altitude and velocity values and the maximum altitude and its corresponding time.

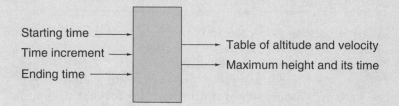

3.   HAND EXAMPLE

Assume that the starting time is 0 hours, the time increment is 1 hour, and the ending time is 5 hours. To obtain the correct units, we need to divide the velocity value in meters/hour by 3600 in order to get meters/sec. Using a calculator, we can then compute the following values:

Time	Altitude (m)	Velocity(m/s)
0	220.00	1.14
1	3,951.88	0.94
2	6,994.08	0.76
3	9,414.28	0.59
4	11,277.28	0.45
5	12,645.00	0.32

We can also determine the maximum altitude from this table, which is 12,645.00 meters; it occurred at 5 hours.

4.   ALGORITHM DEVELOPMENT

We first develop the decomposition outline because it breaks the solution into a series of sequential steps.

Decomposition Outline:

1. *Get user input to specify times for the table.*
2. *Generate and print conversion table, and find maximum height and corresponding time.*
3. *Print maximum height and corresponding time.*

The second step in the decomposition outline represents a loop in which we generate the table and, at the same time, keep track of the maximum height. As we refine this outline, and particularly step 2 into more detail, we need to think carefully about finding the maximum height. Look back at the hand example. Once the table has been printed, it is easy to look at it and select the maximum height. However, when the computer is computing and printing the table, it does not have all the data at one time; it has only the information for the current line in the table. Therefore, to keep track of the maximum, we need to specify a separate variable to store the maximum value. Each time that we compute a new height, we will compare that value to the maximum value. If the new value is larger, we replace the maximum with this new value. We will also need to keep track of the corresponding time. The following refinement in pseudocode outlines these new steps:

Refinement in Pseudocode:

main: *read initial, increment, final values from keyboard*
        set max_height to zero
        set max_time to zero
        print table heading
        set time to initial
        while time<=final
            compute height and velocity
            print height and velocity
            if height>max_height
                set max_height to height
                set max_time to time
            add increment to time
        print max_time and max_height

The steps in the pseudocode are now detailed enough to convert into C. Note that we convert the velocity from meters/hour to meters/second in the `printf` statement.

```
/*-------------------------------------------------------*/
/*   Program chapter3_4                                  */
/*                                                       */
/*   This program prints a table of height and           */
/*   velocity values for a weather balloon.              */

#include <stdio.h>
#include <stdlib.h>
#include <math.h>
```

```
main()
{

   /*  Declare and initialize variables.  */
   double initial, increment, final, time, height,
          velocity, max_time=0, max_height=0;

   /*  Get user input.  */
   printf("Enter initial value for table (in hours): ");
   scanf("%lf",&initial);
   printf("Enter increment between lines (in hours): ");
   scanf("%lf",&increment);
   printf("Enter final value for table (in hours): ");
   scanf("%lf",&final);

   /*  Print report heading.  */
   printf("\n\nWeather Balloon Information \n");
   printf("Time     Height     Velocity \n");
   printf("(hrs)    (meters)   (meters/s) \n");

   /*  Compute and print report information.  */
   for (time=initial; time<=final; time+=increment)
   {
      height = -0.12*pow(time,4) + 12*pow(time,3)
               - 380*time*time + 4100*time + 220;
      velocity = -0.48*pow(time,3) + 36*time*time
               - 760*time + 4100;
      printf("%5.2f  %8.2f    %7.2f \n",
             time,height,velocity/3600);
      if (height > max_height)
      {
         max_height = height;
         max_time = time;
      }
   }

   /*  Print maximum height and corresponding time.  */
   printf("\nMaximum balloon height was %8.2f meters \n",
          max_height);
   printf("and it occurred at %6.2f hours \n",max_time);

   /*  Exit program.  */
   return EXIT_SUCCESS;
}
/*------------------------------------------------------*/
```

5.   TESTING

If we use the data from the hand example, we have the following interaction
with the program:

```
Enter initial value for table (in hours): 0
Enter increment between lines (in hours): 1
Enter final value for table (in hours): 5

Weather Balloon Information
Time      Height     Velocity
(hrs)     (meters)   (meters/s)
 0.00      220.00      1.14
 1.00     3951.88      0.94
 2.00     6994.08      0.76
 3.00     9414.28      0.59
 4.00    11277.28      0.45
 5.00    12645.00      0.32

Maximum balloon height was 12645.00 meters
and it occurred at    5.00 hours
```

Figure 3.7 contains a plot of the altitude and velocity of the balloon for a period of 48 hours. From the plots, we can see the periods during which the balloon rises or falls.

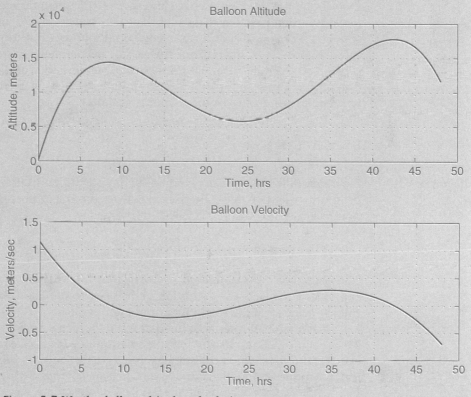

Figure 3.7 *Weather balloon altitude and velocity.*

3.6 Data Files

Engineering problem solutions often involve large amounts of data. These data can be generated by the program as output, or they can be input data used by the program. It is not generally feasible either to print large amounts of data to the screen or to read large amounts of data from the keyboard. In these cases, we usually use **data files** to store the data. These data files are similar to the program files that we create to store our C programs. In fact, a C program file is an input data file to the C compiler and the object program is an output file from the C compiler. In this section we discuss the C statements for interacting with data files and give examples that generate and read information from data files.

When debugging programs that read information from data files, echo (or print) the information read from the file to be sure that the data are being read properly. If the data values are all zero, or are unusual numbers, it may be possible that the program cannot find the file because it is in a directory that the program cannot access. The solution is either to move the file to a directory that the program can access or to change some of the operating system parameters so that the program can find the file.

In the examples that follow, we use data files containing sensor data. For this discussion, we assume that the sensor is a **seismometer**. Seismometers are usually buried near the surface of the earth and record earth motion. These sensors are very sensitive and can record tidal motion even though they may be located hundreds of miles from the ocean. Seismometer data are collected from sensors all over the earth, and are sent by satellite to central locations for collection and analysis. By studying this motion, scientists and engineers may be able to predict earthquakes from seismometer data.

I/O STATEMENTS

File pointer

Each data file used in a program must have a **file pointer** associated with it. If a program uses two files, then each file requires a different file pointer. A file pointer is defined with a **FILE** declaration, as in

```
FILE *sensor1;
```

The **FILE** data type is defined in the header file **stdio.h**; thus, the word **FILE** is capitalized to match the definition in the header file. The asterisk before the identifier specifies that the identifier is a pointer.

After a file pointer is defined, it must then be associated with a specific file. The **fopen** function obtains the information needed to assign a file pointer to a specific file. The two arguments for this function are the file name and a character that indicates the file status, which is also called the **file open mode**; both the file name and the character need to be enclosed in double quotes. If we are going to read information from a file with a program, the file open mode is **r** for

File open mode

read. If we are going to write information to a file with a program, the file open mode is **w** for write. Thus, the following statement specifies that the file pointer **sensor1** is going to be used with a file named **sensor1.dat** from which we will read information:

```
sensor1 = fopen("sensor1.dat","r");
```

Once an input file and its pointer have been specified, we can read information from it, much as we would read information from the keyboard. However, instead of using the **scanf** function, we use the **fscanf** function. If each line in the **sensor1.dat** file contains a time and sensor reading, we can read one line of this information and store the values in the variables **time** and **motion** with this statement:

```
fscanf(sensor1,"%lf %lf",&time,&motion);
```

Note that the difference between the **scanf** function and the **fscanf** function is that the first argument in the **fscanf** function is the file pointer. Otherwise, both statements are the same. The **scanf** statement converts the characters received from the keyboard to values, and the **fscanf** statement converts the characters from the lines in the data file to values.

If the file is an output file, we can write information to the file with the **fprintf** function. The first argument of the **fprintf** statement is the file pointer, and the rest of the arguments define the variables and the form in which the corresponding values are to be written in the file. For example, consider the program developed earlier in this chapter that computed and printed a table of time, altitude, and velocity data. If we wanted to modify this program so that it generated a data file containing this set of data, we could use a pointer **balloon** that would be associated with an output file named **ballon.dat** using these statements:

```
FILE *balloon;
...
balloon = fopen("balloon.dat","w");
```

Then, as we compute the time, altitude, and velocity information, we can write it to the file with this statement:

```
fprintf(balloon,"%f %f %f\n",
        time,height,velocity/3600);
```

The newline indicator causes a skip to a new line after each group of three values is written to the file.

The **fclose** function is used to close a file after we are finished with it; the function argument is the file pointer. To close the two files used in these example statements, we use the following statements:

```
fclose(sensor1);
fclose(balloon);
```

There is no distinction between closing an input file and closing an output file. If a file has not been closed when the **return EXIT_SUCCESS** statement is executed, it will automatically be closed.

A preprocessor directive is often used to specify the data file name because we frequently use the same program with different data files. It is easier to modify the preprocessor directive than it is to search through the statements for the **fopen** function. An example of a preprocessor directive and a corresponding **fopen** function are the following:

```
#define FILENAME "sensor1.dat"
...
sensor1 = fopen(FILENAME,"r");
```

This combination of statements is used in all the example programs that use files in this and the following chapters. Because some operating systems are case-sensitive, we will use all lowercase letters in file names to avoid any potential problems.

READING DATA FILES

In order to read information from a data file, we must first know some details about the file. Obviously we must know the file name so that we can use the **fopen** statement to associate the file with its pointer. We must also know the order and data type of the values stored in the file so that we can declare corresponding identifiers correctly. Finally, we need to know if there is any special information in the file to help us determine how much information is in the file. If we attempt to execute an **fscanf** statement after we have read all the data in the file, an error occurs. In order to avoid this error, we need to know when we have read all the data.

Data files generally have one of three common structures. Some files have been generated so that the first line in the file contains the number of lines (also called **records**) with information that follow. For example, suppose that a file containing sensor data has 150 sets of time and sensor information. The data file could be constructed so that the first line contains only the value 150; that line would then be followed by 150 lines containing the sensor data. To read the data from this file, we read the value from the first line in the file and then use a **for** loop to read the rest of the information. This type of loop is also called a **counter-controlled loop**.

Another form of file structure uses a **trailer** or **sentinel signal**. These signals are special data values that are used to indicate or signal the last record of a file. For example, the sensor data file constructed with a sentinel signal would contain the 150 lines of information followed by a line with special values, such as −999.0 for the time and sensor value. These sentinel signals must be values that could not appear as regular data in order to avoid confusion. To read data from this type of file, we use a **while** loop with a condition that is true as long as the data value is not the sentinel signal. This type of loop is called a **sentinel-controlled loop**.

Records

Counter-controlled loop

Sentinel-controlled loop

The third data file structure contains only valid data; it does not contain an initial line with the number of valid data records that follow, and it does not contain a trailer or sentinel signal. For this type of data file, we use the value returned by the **fscanf** function to help us determine when we have read the last line of the file. To read data from this type of file, we use a **while** loop with a condition that is true as long as we are not at the end of the file.

We now present programs for reading sensor information and printing a summary report that contains the number of sensor readings, the average value, the maximum value, and the minimum value. Each of the three common file formats discussed will be used in the following programs.

Specified Number of Records. Assume that the first record in the data file **sensor1.dat** contains an integer that specifies the number of records of sensor information that follow. Each following line contains a time and sensor reading, as shown below:

```
10
0.0   132.5
0.1   147.2
0.2   148.3
0.3   157.3
0.4   163.2
0.5   158.2
0.6   169.3
0.7   148.2
0.8   137.6
0.9   135.9
```

The process of first reading the number of data points and then using that to specify the number of times to read data and accumulate information is easily described using a variable-controlled loop. In the following program, the first actual data value is used to initialize the **maximum** and **minimum** values. If we set the **minimum** value initially to zero and all the sensor values were greater than zero, the program would print the erroneous value of zero for the minimum sensor reading.

```
/*-----------------------------------------------------------*/
/*  Program chapter3_5                                       */
/*                                                           */
/*  This program generates a summary report from            */
/*  a data file that has the number of data points          */
/*  in the first record.                                     */

#include <stdio.h>
#include <stdlib.h>
#define FILENAME "sensor1.dat"

main()
{
   /*  Declare and initialize variables.  */
   int num_data_pts, k;
```

```
      double time, motion, sum=0, maximum, minimum;
      FILE *sensor1;

      /*  Open file and read the number of data points.  */
      sensor1 = fopen(FILENAME,"r");
      fscanf(sensor1,"%i",&num_data_pts);

      /*  Read data and compute summary information.  */
      for (k=1; k<=num_data_pts; k++)
      {
         fscanf(sensor1,"%lf %lf",&time,&motion);
         if (k == 1)
            maximum = minimum = motion;
         sum += motion;
         if (motion > maximum)
            maximum = motion;
         if (motion < minimum)
            minimum = motion;
      }

      /*  Print summary information.  */
      printf("Number of sensor readings: %i \n",
             num_data_pts);
      printf("Average reading:           %.2f \n",
             sum/num_data_pts);
      printf("Maximum reading:           %.2f \n",maximum);
      printf("Minimum reading:           %.2f \n",minimum);

      /*  Close file and exit program.  */
      fclose(sensor1);
      return EXIT_SUCCESS;
   }
/*-------------------------------------------------------*/
```

The report printed by this program is the following:

```
Number of sensor readings: 10
Average reading:           149.77
Maximum reading:           169.30
Minimum reading:           132.50
```

Trailer or Sentinel Signals. Assume that the data file **sensor2.dat** contains the same information as the **sensor1.dat** file, but instead of giving the number of valid data records at the beginning of the file, a final record contains a trailer signal. The time value on last line in the file will contain a negative value, so we know that it is not a valid line of information. A second number must be included on the trailer line because the statement that reads each line expects two values; otherwise an error occurs. The contents of the data file are as follows:

```
0.0    132.5
0.1    147.2
0.2    148.3
0.3    157.3
0.4    163.2
0.5    158.2
0.6    169.3
0.7    148.2
0.8    137.6
0.9    135.9
-99    -99
```

The process of reading and accumulating information until we read the trailer signal is easily described using a do/while loop structure as shown in the following program.

```
/*-----------------------------------------------------*/
/*  Program chapter3_6                                 */
/*                                                     */
/*  This program generates a summary report from       */
/*  a data file that has a trailer record with        */
/*  negative values.                                   */

#include <stdio.h>
#include <stdlib.h>
#define FILENAME "sensor2.dat"

main()
{
   /*  Declare and initialize variables.  */
   int num_data_pts=0, k;
   double time, motion, sum=0, maximum, minimum;
   FILE *sensor2;

   /*  Open file and read the first data point.  */
   sensor2 = fopen(FILENAME,"r");
   fscanf(sensor2,"%lf %lf",&time,&motion);

   /*  Initialize variables using first data point.  */
   maximum = minimum = motion;

   /*  Update summary data until trailer record read.  */
   do
   {
      sum += motion;
      if (motion > maximum)
         maximum = motion;
      if (motion < minimum)
         minimum = motion;
      num_data_pts++;
      fscanf(sensor2,"%lf %lf",&time,&motion);
   } while (time >= 0);
```

```
              /*  Print summary information.  */
              printf("Number of sensor readings: %i \n",
                     num_data_pts);
              printf("Average reading:           %.2f \n",
                     sum/num_data_pts);
              printf("Maximum reading:           %.2f \n",maximum);
              printf("Minimum reading:           %.2f \n",minimum);

              /*  Close file and exit program.  */
              fclose(sensor2);
              return EXIT_SUCCESS;
       }
       /*-------------------------------------------------------*/
```

The report printed by this program using the **sensor2.dat** file is exactly the same as the report printed using the **sensor1.dat** file.

End-of-file indicator

End-of-File. A special **end-of-file indicator** is inserted at the end of every data file; the **feof** function in the Standard C library can be used to detect when this indicator has been reached in a data file. The **fscanf** function can also be used to detect when the end of the data has been reached in a file. Recall that the **fscanf** function returns the number of values successfully read each time that it is executed. Thus, if the function returns a value that is different from the number of values that it was supposed to read, the end of the data file has been reached or there are errors in the information in the data file. If the information in the data file is valid, the **fscanf** function can be used to determine when the end of the data file is reached. Consider the following statements:

```
       while ((fscanf(data1,"%f",&x)) == 1)
       {
          count++;
          sum += x;
       }
       ave = sum/count;
```

The **fscanf** function attempts to read a value for **x** from a data file. If a value is read, the function returns a value of 1, and the statements within the loop are executed. If the end of the data file is reached, there are no more data; thus the function does not return a value of 1, and control passes to the statement following the **while** loop.

We now assume that the data file **sensor3.dat** contains the same information as the **sensor2.dat** file except that it does not include the trailer signal. The contents of the data file are shown below:

```
       0.0   132.5
       0.1   147.2
       0.2   148.3
       0.3   157.3
       0.4   163.2
       0.5   158.2
       0.6   169.3
```

```
0.7   148.2
0.8   137.6
0.9   135.9
```

In the following program we read and accumulate information until we reach the
end of the data file.

```c
/*--------------------------------------------------------*/
/*  Program chapter3_7                                    */
/*                                                        */
/*  This program generates a summary report from          */
/*  a data file that does not have a header record        */
/*  or a trailer record.                                   */

#include <stdio.h>
#include <stdlib.h>
#define FILENAME "sensor3.dat"

main()
{
   /*  Declare and initialize variables.  */
   int num_data_pts=0, k;
   double time, motion, sum=0, maximum, minimum;
   FILE *sensor3;

   /*  Open file.  */
   sensor3 = fopen(FILENAME,"r");

   /*  While not at the end of the file, */
   /*  read and accumulate information.  */
   while ((fscanf(sensor3,"%lf %lf",&time,&motion)) == 2)
   {
      num_data_pts++;
      if (num_data_pts == 1)
         maximum = minimum = motion;
      sum += motion;
      if (motion > maximum)
         maximum = motion;
      if (motion < minimum)
         minimum== = motion;
   }

   /*  Print summary information.  */
   printf("Number of sensor readings: %i \n",
          num_data_pts);
   printf("Average reading:           %.2f \n",
          sum/num_data_pts);
   printf("Maximum reading:           %.2f \n",maximum);
   printf("Minimum reading:           %.2f \n",minimum);

   /*  Close file and exit program.  */
   fclose(sensor3);
   return EXIT_SUCCESS;
}
/*--------------------------------------------------------*/
```

The program printed the same report as those printed by the two previous programs.

The programs in this section work properly if the data files exist and contain the information expected. An error would occur if the program attempted to open a file that did not exist, and a division by zero error would occur if the number of points were zero.

All three file structures are commonly used in engineering and scientific applications. Therefore, it is important to know which type of structure is used when you work with a data file. If you make the wrong assumption, you may get incorrect answers instead of an error message. Sometimes the only way to be sure of the file structure is to print the first few lines and the last few lines of the file.

GENERATING A DATA FILE

Generating a data file is very similar to printing a report; instead of writing the line to the terminal screen, we write it to a data file. Before we generate the data file, though, we must decide what file structure we want to use. In the previous discussion, we presented the three most common file structures—files with an initial record giving the number of valid records that follow, files with a trailer or sentinel record to indicate the end of the valid data, and files with only valid data records and no special beginning or ending records.

There are advantages and disadvantages to each of the three file structures discussed. A file with a trailer signal is simple to use, but choosing a value for the trailer signal must be done carefully so that it does not contain values that could occur in the valid data. If the first record in the data file will contain the number of lines of actual data, we must know how many lines of data will be in the file before we begin to generate the file. It may not always be easy to determine the number of lines before executing the program that generates the file. The simplest file to generate is the one that contains only the valid information, with no special information at the beginning or end of the file. If the information in the file is going to be used with a plotting package, it is usually best to use this third file structure, which includes only valid information.

We now present a program that is a modification of the program presented earlier in the chapter that printed a table of time, altitude, and velocity values for a weather balloon. In addition to generating a table of information that is displayed on the screen, we also write the information to a data file. Compare this program to the one in section 3.5 on page 81.

```
/*-----------------------------------------------------*/
/*   Program chapter3_8                                 */
/*                                                      */
/*   This program generates a file of height and       */
/*   velocity values for a weather balloon. The        */
/*   information is also printed in a report.           */
```

```c
#include <stdio.h>
#include <stdlib.h>
#include <math.h>
#define FILENAME "balloon.dat"

main()
{
   /*  Declare and initialize variables.  */
   double initial, increment, final, time, height,
          velocity, max_time=0, max_height=0;
   FILE *balloon;

   /*  Open output file.  */
   balloon = fopen(FILENAME,"w");

   /*  Get user input.  */
   printf("Enter initial value for table (in hours): ");
   scanf("%lf",&initial);
   printf("Enter increment between lines (in hours): ");
   scanf("%lf",&increment);
   printf("Enter final value for table (in hours): ");
   scanf("%lf",&final);

   /*  Print report heading.  */
   printf("\n\nWeather Balloon Information \n");
   printf("Time      Height      Velocity \n");
   printf("(hrs)    (meters)   (meters/s) \n");

   /*  Compute and print report information  */
   /*  and write data to a file.             */
   for (time=initial; time<=final; time+=increment)
   {
      height = -0.12*pow(time,4) + 12*pow(time,3)
               - 380*time*time + 4100*time + 220;
      velocity = -0.48*pow(time,3) + 36*time*time
                 - 760*time + 4100;
      printf("%6.2f  %8.2f   %7.2f \n",
             time,height,velocity/3600);
      fprintf(balloon,"%.2f %.2f %.2f \n",
              time,height,velocity/3600);
      if (height > max_height)
      {
         max_height = height;
         max_time = time;
      }
   }
   /*  Print maximum height and corresponding time.  */
   printf("\nMaximum balloon height was %8.2f meters \n",
          max_height);
   printf("and it occurred at %6.2f hours \n",max_time);

   /*  Close file and exit program.  */
   fclose(balloon);
   return EXIT_SUCCESS;
}
/*-------------------------------------------------------*/
```

The first few lines of a data file generated by this program using an initial time of 0 hours, an increment of 0.5 hours, and a final time of 48 hours are

```
0.00 220.00 1.14
0.50 2176.49 1.04
1.00 3951.88 0.94
1.50 5554.89 0.84
...
```

A plot of this specific file was shown in Figure 3.7 on page 83.

CHAPTER SUMMARY

In this chapter we covered the use of conditions and **if** statements to select the proper statements to be executed. We also presented techniques for repeating sets of statements that used loops. These loops can be implemented as **while** loops or **for** loops. These selection and repetition structures are used in most programs. In addition, we included the statements necessary to read information from a data file so that we could use the information in the program. We also presented the statements to generate a data file from a program. Data files are commonly used in solving engineering problems; therefore, this concept was presented early in the text so that we could use it in many of the later problem solutions.

KEY TERMS

compound statement

condition

data file

decomposition outline

divide and conquer

empty statement

end-of-file indicator

file open mode

file pointer

flowchart

infinite loop

iteration

logical operator

loop

loop-control variable

pseudocode

record

relational operator

repetition

selection

sequence

sentinel signal

stepwise refinement

top-down design

trailer signal

C STATEMENT SUMMARY

Declaration for file pointer

```
FILE *sensor1;
```

if statement

```
if (temp > 100)
    printf("Temperature exceeds limit \n");
```

if/else statement

```
if (d <= 30)
    velocity = 4.25 + 0.00175*d*d;
else
    velocity = 0.65 + 0.12*d - 0.0025*d*d;
```

while loop

```
while (degrees <= 360)
{
    radians = degrees*PI/180;
    printf("%6.0f %9.6f \n",degrees,radians);
    degrees += 10;
}
```

do/while loop

```
do
{
    radians = degrees*PI/180;
    printf("%6.0f %9.6f \n",degrees,radians);
    degrees += 10;
} while (degrees <= 360);
```

for loop

```
for (degrees=0; degrees<=360; degrees+=10)
{
    radians = degrees*PI/180;
    printf("%6.0f %9.6f \n",degrees,radians);
}
```

break statement

```
break;
```

continue statement

```
continue;
```

File open function

```
sensor1 = fopen("sensor1.dat","r");
balloon = fopen(FILENAME,"w");
```

File input function

```
fscanf(sensor1,"%lf %lf",&t,&motion);
```

File output function

```
fprintf(balloon,"%f %f %f\n",
        time,altitude,velocity/3600);
```

File close function

```
fclose(sensor1);
```

Style NOTES

1. Use spaces around the relational operator in a logical expression in a simple condition; use spaces around the logical operator and not around the relational operators in a complicated condition.
2. Indent the statements within a compound statement or inside a loop. If loops or compound statements are nested, indent each nested set of statements from the previous statement.
3. Use braces to clearly identify blocks of statements when there could be confusion in interpretation of nested loops.
4. Define filenames with preprocessor directives so that they can easily be changed.

DEBUGGING NOTES

1. Be sure to use the relational operator == instead of = in a condition for equality.
2. Put the braces surrounding a block of statements on lines by themselves; this will help you avoid omitting one of them.
3. Do not use the equality operator with floating-point values; instead, test for values "close to" a desired value.
4. Recompile your program frequently when correcting syntax errors; correcting one error may remove many error messages.
5. Use the `printf` statement to give memory snapshots of the values of key variables when debugging loops.
6. It is easier than you think to generate an infinite loop; be sure you know the special characters needed to abort the execution of a program on your system if it goes into an infinite loop.

7. When debugging a program that reads data from a data file, print the values as soon as they are read to check for errors in reading the information.

8. When debugging a program that reads a data file, be sure that your program can access the directory that contains the data file.

9. To avoid problems with operating systems that are not case-sensitive, use filenames with lowercase letters.

PROBLEMS

Unit Conversions. The following problems generate tables of unit conversions. Include a table heading and column headings for the tables. Choose the number of decimal places based on the values to be printed.

1. Generate a table of conversions from degrees to radians. The first line should contain the value for $0°$, and the last line should contain the values for $360°$. Allow the user to enter the increment to use between lines in the table.

2. Generate a table of conversions from mi/hr to ft/s. Start the mi/hr column at 0, and increment by 5 mi/hr. The last line should contain the value 65 mi/hr. (Recall that 1 mi = 5280 ft.)

Currency Conversions. The following problems generate tables of currency conversions. Use title and column headings. Assume the following conversion rates:

1 dollar ($) = 5.045 francs (Fr)

1 yen (Y)   = $ 0.010239

1 dollar ($) − 1.4685 deutsche marks (DM)

3. Generate a table of conversions from francs to dollars. Start the francs column at 5 Fr, and increment by 5 Fr. Print 25 lines in the table.

4. Generate a table of conversions from yen to deutsche marks. Start the yen column at 100 Y and print 25 lines, with the final line containing the value 10000 Y.

Temperature Conversions. The following problems generate temperature conversion tables. Use the following equations that give relationships between temperatures in degrees Fahrenheit (T_F), degrees Celsius (T_C), degrees Kelvin (T_K), and degrees Rankin (T_R):

$$T_F = T_R - 459.67° \text{ R}$$

$$T_F = \left(\frac{9}{5}\right)T_C + 32° \text{ F}$$

$$T_R = \left(\frac{9}{5}\right)T_K$$

5. Write a program to generate a table of conversions from Fahrenheit to Kelvin for values from 0°F to 200°F. Allow the user to enter the increment in degrees Fahrenheit between lines.

6. Write a program to generate a table of conversions from Celsius to Rankin. Allow the user to enter the starting temperature and increment between lines. Print 25 lines in the table.

Suture Packaging. Sutures are strands or fibers used to sew living tissue together after an injury or an operation. Packages of sutures must be sealed carefully before they are shipped to hospitals so that contaminants cannot enter the packages. The object that seals the package is referred to as a sealing die. Generally, sealing dies are heated with an electric heater. For the sealing process to be a success, the sealing die is maintained at an established temperature and must contact the package with a predetermined pressure for an established time period. The time period in which the sealing die contacts the package is called the dwell time. Assume that the acceptable range of parameters for an acceptable seal are the following:

Temperature:	150–170° C
Pressure:	60–70 psi
Dwell time:	2–2.5 s

7. A data file named **suture.dat** contains information on batches of sutures that have been rejected during a one-week period. Each line in the data file contains the batch number, the temperature, the pressure, and the dwell time for a rejected batch. The quality control engineer would like to analyze this information and needs a report that computes the percent of the batches rejected due to temperature, the percent rejected due to pressure, and the percent rejected due to dwell time. It is possible that a specific batch may have been rejected for more than one reason and should be counted in all applicable totals. Write a program to compute and print these three percentages. Use the following test data:

Batch Number	Temperature	Pressure	Dwell Time
24551	145.5	62.3	2.23
24582	153.7	63.2	2.52
26553	160.3	58.9	2.51
26623	159.5	58.9	2.01
26642	160.3	61.2	1.98

8. Write a program to read the data file **suture.dat** from problem 7. Make sure that the information relates only to batches that should have been rejected. If any batch should not be in the data file, print an appropriate message with the batch information. Test your program with the specified data file; then insert records with information that should not have been rejected to be sure your program will identify these records.

Timber Regrowth. A problem in timber management is to determine how much of an area to leave uncut so that the harvested area is reforested in a certain period of time. It is assumed that reforestation takes place at a known rate per year, depending on climate and soil conditions. A reforestation equation expresses this growth as a function of the amount of timber standing and the reforestation rate. For example, if 100 acres are left standing after harvesting and the reforestation rate is 0.05, then $100 + 0.05 \times 100$, or 105 acres, are forested at the end of the first year. At the end of the second year, the number of acres forested is $105 + 0.05 \times 105$, or 110.25 acres. Test your program with the specified data file; then insert records with information that should not have been rejected to be sure your

9. Assume that there are 14,000 acres total with 2500 acres uncut and that the reforestation rate is 0.02. Print a table showing the number of acres reforested at the end of each year, for a total of 20 years.

10. Modify the program developed in problem 9 so that the user can enter a number of acres and the program will determine how many years are required for that number of acres to be completely reforested.

4

Courtesy of Chevron Corporation.

GRAND CHALLENGE:
Enhanced Oil and Gas Recovery

The design and construction of the Alaskan pipeline presented numerous engineering challenges. One of the important problems that had to be addressed was protecting the permafrost (the permanently frozen subsoil in arctic or subarctic regions) from the heat of the pipeline itself. The oil flowing in the pipeline is warmed by pumping stations and by friction from the walls of the pipe, so the supports holding the pipeline must be insulated or even cooled to keep them from melting the permafrost at their bases. In addition, the components of the pipeline had to be very reliable because of the inaccessibility of some locations. More importantly, component failure could cause damage to human life, animal life, and the environment around the pipeline.

Modular Programming with Functions

4.1   Modularity

4.2   Programmer-Defined Functions

Chapter Summary, Key Terms, C Statement Summary
Style Notes, Debugging Notes, Problems

OBJECTIVES

In this chapter, we discuss the importance of dividing programs into functions (or modules) that perform specific operations. In C, modules are available from libraries, such as the Standard C library. Programmer-defined modules may also be written specifically to accompany a `main` function. This chapter presents several examples of programmer-written functions.

4.1   Modularity

Modules

The execution of a C program begins with the statements in the `main` function. A program may also contain other functions, and it may refer to functions in another file or in a library. These functions, or **modules**, are sets of statements that typically perform an operation or that compute a value. For example, the `printf` function prints a line of information on the terminal screen, and the `sqrt` function computes the square root of a value.

Style

To maintain simplicity and readability in longer and more complex problem solutions, we develop programs that use a `main` function plus additional functions, instead of using one long `main` function. *By separating a solution into a group of modules, each module is simpler and easier to understand, thus adhering to the basic guidelines of structured programming presented in Chapter 3.*

The process of developing a problem solution is often one of "divide and conquer," as was discussed when we first discussed the decomposition outline. Because the decomposition outline is a set of sequentially executed steps that solve the problem, it provides a good starting point for selecting potential functions. In fact, it is not uncommon for each step in the decomposition outline to correspond to one or more function references in the `main` function.

Breaking a problem solution into a set of modules has many advantages. Because a module has a specific purpose, it can be written and tested separately from the rest of the problem solution. An individual module is smaller than the complete solution, so testing it is easier. And, once a module has been carefully tested, it can be used in new problem solutions without being retested. For example, suppose that a module is developed to find the average of a group of values. Once this module is written and tested, it can be used in other programs that need to compute an average. This **reusability** is a very important issue in the development of large software systems because it can save development time. In fact, libraries of commonly used modules (such as the Standard C library) are often available on computer systems.

Reusability

The use of modules (called **modularity**) often reduces the overall length of a program, because many problem solutions include steps that are repeated several places in the program. By incorporating these steps that are repeated in a function, the steps can be referenced with a single statement each time they are needed.

Several programmers can work on the same project if it is separated into modules because the individual modules can be developed and tested independently of each other. This allows the development schedule to be accelerated because some of the work can be done in parallel.

Abstraction

The use of modules that have been written to accomplish specific tasks supports the concept of **abstraction**. The modules contain the details of the tasks, and the programmer can reference the modules without worrying about these details. The I/O diagrams that we use in developing a problem solution are an example of abstraction—we specify the input information and the output information without giving the details of how the output information is determined. In a similar way, we can think of modules as "black boxes" that have a specified input and compute specified information. We can use these modules to help develop a solution; thus, we are able to operate at a higher level of abstraction to solve problems. For example, the Standard C library contains functions that compute the logarithms of values. We can reference these functions without being concerned about the specific details, such as whether the functions are using infinite series approximations or look-up tables to compute the specified logarithms. By using abstraction, we can reduce the development time of software as we increase its quality.

To summarize, some of the advantages of using modules in a problem solution are the following:

- A module can be written and tested separately from other parts of the solution; thus, module development can be done in parallel for large projects.

- A module is a small part of the solution; thus, testing it separately is easier.

- Once a module is tested carefully, it does not need to be retested before it can be used in new problem solutions.

- The use of modules usually reduces the length of a program, making it more readable.

- The use of modules promotes the concept of abstraction, which allows the programmer to "hide" the details in modules. This allows us to use modules in a functional sense without being concerned about the specific details.

Additional benefits of modules will be pointed out as we progress through this chapter.

As we begin to develop solutions to more complicated problems, the programs become longer. Therefore, we include here three suggestions for debugging longer programs. First, it is sometimes helpful to run a program using a different compiler because different compilers have different error messages. In fact some compilers have extensive error messages, whereas others give very little information about some errors. Another useful step in debugging a long program is to add comment indicators (/* and */) around some sections of the code so that you can focus on other parts of the program. Of course, you must be careful that you do not comment out statements that affect variables needed for the parts of the program that you want to test. Finally, test complicated functions by themselves. This is usually done with a special program called a **driver** whose purpose is to provide a simple interface between you and the function that you are testing. Typically, this program asks you to enter the parameters that you want passed to the function, and it then prints the value returned by the function.

4.2   Programmer-Defined Functions

Invoked

The execution of a program always begins with the **main** function. Additional functions are called, or **invoked**, when the program encounters function names. These additional functions must be defined in the file containing the **main** function or in another available file or library of files. (If the function is included in a system library file, such as the Standard C library, it is often called a **library function**; other functions are usually called **programmer-written** or **programmer-defined functions**.) After executing the statements in a function, the program execution continues with the statement that called the function.

FUNCTION DEFINITION

The sinc(x) function, plotted in Figure 4.1, is commonly used in many engineering applications. The most common definition for sinc(x) is the following:

$$f(x) = \text{sinc}(x)$$

$$= \frac{\sin(x)}{x}$$

(The sinc(x) function is also occasionally defined as $\sin(\pi x)/\pi x$.) The values of this function can be easily computed except for sinc(0), which gives an indeterminant form of 0/0. In this case, L'Hopital's theorem from calculus can be used to prove that sinc(0) = 1.

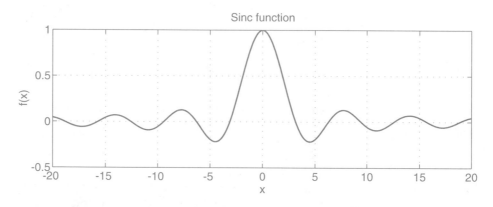

Figure 4.1 *Sinc function in [−20,20].*

Assume that we want to develop a program that allows the user to enter interval limits, a and b. The program should then compute and print 21 values of sinc(x) for values of x evenly spaced between a and b, inclusively. Thus, the first value of x should be a. An increment should then be added to obtain the next value of x, and so on, until the 21st value, which should be b. Therefore, the increment in x is

$$x\_\text{increment} = \frac{\text{interval width}}{20}$$

$$= \frac{b - a}{20}$$

Select values for a and b, and convince yourself that, with this increment, and with a as the first value, the 21st value will be b.

Because sinc(x) is not part of the mathematical functions provided by the Standard C library, we implement this problem solution two ways. In one solution we include the statements to perform the computations of sinc(x) in the **main** function; in the other solution we write a programmer-defined function to compute sinc(x) and then reference the programmer-defined function each time that the computations are needed. Both solutions are now presented so that you can compare them.

SOLUTION 1

```
/*-------------------------------------------------------*/
/*  Program chapter4_1                                   */
/*                                                       */
/*  This program prints 21 values of the sinc            */
/*  function in the interval [a,b] using                 */
/*  computations within the main function.               */

#include <stdio.h>
#include <stdlib.h>
#include <math.h>

main()
{
    /*  Declare variables.  */
    int k;
    double a, b, x_incr, new_x, sinc_x;

    /*  Get interval endpoints from the user.  */
    printf("Enter end points a and b (a<b): \n");
    scanf("%lf %lf",&a,&b);
    x_incr = (b - a)/20;

    /*  Compute and print table of sinc(x) values.  */
    printf("x and sinc(x) \n");
    for (k=0; k<=20; k++)
    {
        new_x = a + k*x_incr;
        if (fabs(new_x) < 0.0001)
            sinc_x = 1.0;
        else
            sinc_x = sin(new_x)/new_x;
        printf("%f %f \n",new_x,sinc_x);
    }

    /*  Exit program.  */
    return EXIT_SUCCESS;
}
/*-------------------------------------------------------*/
```

We now present a second solution that uses a programmer-defined function to compute values of sinc(x).

SOLUTION 2

```c
/*-----------------------------------------------------*/
/*  Program chapter4_2                                 */
/*                                                     */
/*  This program prints 21 values of the sinc          */
/*  function in the interval [a,b] using a             */
/*  programmer-defined function.                       */
/*                                                     */

#include <stdio.h>
#include <stdlib.h>
#include <math.h>

main()
{
   /*  Declare variables and function prototypes.  */
   int k;
   double a, b, x_incr, new_x;
   double sinc(double x);

   /*  Get interval endpoints from the user.  */
   printf("Enter endpoints a and b, (a<b): \n");
   scanf("%lf %lf",&a,&b);
   x_incr = (b - a)/20;

   /*  Compute and print table of sinc(x) values.  */
   printf("x and sinc(x) \n");
   for (k=0; k<=20; k++)
   {
      new_x = a + k*x_incr;
      printf("%f %f \n",new_x,sinc(new_x));
   }

   /*  Exit program.  */
   return EXIT_SUCCESS;
}
/*-----------------------------------------------------*/
/*  This function evaluates the sinc function.         */
/*                                                     */

double sinc(double x)
{
   if (fabs(x) < 0.0001)
      return 1.0;
   else
      return sin(x)/x;
 }
/*-----------------------------------------------------*/
```

The following output represents an example interaction that could occur with either program:

```
Enter endpoints a and b, (a<b):
-5 5
x and sinc(x)
-5.000000 -0.191785
```

```
-4.500000 -0.217229
-4.000000 -0.189201
-3.500000 -0.100224
-3.000000 0.047040
-2.500000 0.239389
-2.000000 0.454649
-1.500000 0.664997
-1.000000 0.841471
-0.500000 0.958851
0.000000 1.000000
0.500000 0.958851
1.000000 0.841471
1.500000 0.664997
2.000000 0.454649
2.500000 0.239389
3.000000 0.047040
3.500000 -0.100224
4.000000 -0.189201
4.500000 -0.217229
5.000000 -0.191785
```

Figure 4.2 contains plots of the 21 values computed for four different intervals [a, b]. Because the program computes only 21 values, the resolution in the plots is affected by the size of the interval—a smaller interval has better resolution than a

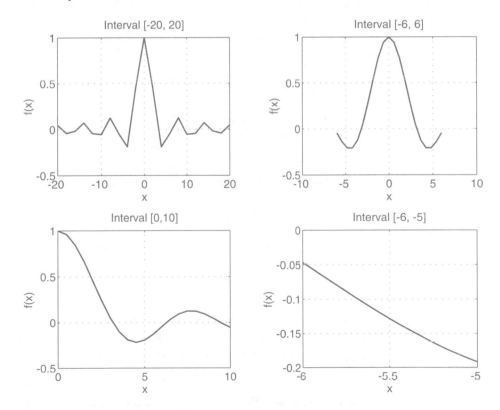

Figure 4.2 *Program output for four intervals.*

larger interval. Now that you have an example of a program with a programmer-defined function, we present a more general discussion of the statements in a function.

A function consists of a definition statement followed by declarations and
statements. The first part of the definition statement defines the type of value that
is returned by the function; if the function does not return a value, the type is
void. The function name and parameter list follow the return_type. Thus, the
general form of a function is

```
return-type function_name(parameter declarations)
{
   declarations;
   statements;
}
```

Style

Style

The parameter declarations represent the information passed to the function. If
there are no input parameters (also called arguments), then the parameter declarations should be **void**. Additional variables used by a function are defined in the
declarations. The declarations and the statements within a function are enclosed
in braces. *The function name should be selected to help document the purpose of
the function.* Comments should also be included within the function to further
describe the purpose of the function and to document the steps. *We also use a
comment line with dashes to separate a programmer-defined function from the
main function and from other programmer-defined functions.*

All functions should include a **return** statement, which has the following
general form:

```
return expression;
```

The expression specifies the value to be returned to the statement that referenced
the function. The expression type should match the return_type indicated in the
function definition to avoid potential errors. The cast operator (discussed in Chapter
2) can be used to explicitly specify the type of the expression if necessary. A **void
function** does not return a value and thus has this general definition statement:

```
void function_name(parameter declarations)
```

The **return** statement in a **void** function does not contain an expression and has
this form:

```
return;
```

Compare the general form of a function that has just been described with the
sinc function defined in program **chapter 4_2**. Also, note that the **main** function
of this solution is easier to read because it is shorter than the **main** function in the
first solution.

Functions can be defined before or after the **main** function. (Remember that
a right brace specifies the end of the **main** function.) However, one function must
be completely defined before another function begins; function definitions cannot

Style

be nested within each other. *In our programs, we include the* main *function first; then additional functions are included in the order in which they are referenced in the program.*

We now look closer at the interaction between a statement that references a function and the function itself.

FUNCTION PROTOTYPE

The **main** function presented in program **chapter4_2** contained the following statement in its declarations:

```
double sinc(double x);
```

Function prototype

This statement is a **function prototype** statement. It informs the compiler that the **main** function will reference a function named **sinc**, that the **sinc** function expects a **double** parameter, and that the **sinc** function returns a **double** value. The identifier **x** is not being defined as a variable; it is just used to indicate that a value is expected as an argument by the **sinc** function. In fact, it is valid to include only the argument types in the function prototype statement:

```
double sinc(double);
```

Style

Both of these prototype statements give the same information to the compiler. *We recommend using parameter identifiers in prototype statements because the identifiers help document the order and definition of the parameters.*

A function prototype can be included with preprocessor directives, or because a function prototype is defining the type of value being returned by the function, it can also be included with other variable declarations. For example, the declarations of program **chapter4_2** are

```
/*  Declare variables and function prototypes.  */
int k;
double a, b, x_incr, new_x;
double sinc(double x);
```

These statements could also have been written in the following form:

```
/*  Declare variables and function prototypes.  */
int k;
double a, b, x_incr, new_x, sinc(double x);
```

Style

In our programs, we list function prototypes on separate declaration statements to make it easier to identify them.

Function prototype statements should be included for all functions referenced in a program. Header files, such as **stdio.h** and **math.h**, contain the prototype statements for many of the functions in the Standard C library. Otherwise, we would need to include individual prototype statements for functions such as **printf** and **sqrt** in our programs. If a programmer-defined function references other programmer-defined functions, it will also need additional prototype statements.

If a program references a large number of programmer-defined functions, it becomes cumbersome to include all the function prototype statements. In these cases, a custom header file can be defined that contains the function prototypes and any related symbolic constants. A header file must have a filename that ends with a suffix of **.h**. The file is then referenced with an **include** statement, using double quotes around the filename. Custom header files are often used to accompany routines that are shared by programmers.

PARAMETER LIST

The definition statement of a function defines the parameters that are required by the function; these are called **formal parameters**. Any statement that references the function must include values that correspond to the parameters; these are called **actual parameters.** For example, consider the **sinc** function developed earlier in this section. The definition statement of this function is

```
double sinc(double x)
```

and the statement from the **main** program that references the function is

```
printf("%f %f \n",new_x,sinc(new_x));
```

Thus, the variable **x** is the formal parameter, and the variable **new_x** is the actual parameter. When the reference to the **sinc** function in the **printf** statement is executed, the value in the actual parameter is copied to the formal parameter, and the steps in the **sinc** function are executed using the new value in **x**. The value returned by the **sinc** function is then printed. It is important to note that the value in the formal parameter is not moved back to the actual parameter when the function is completed. We illustrate these steps with a memory snapshot that shows the transfer of the value from the actual parameter to the formal parameter, assuming that the value of **new_x** is 5.0:

Actual Parameter   Formal Parameter

new_x   [5.0]   →   x   [5.0]

After the value in the actual parameter is copied to the formal parameter, the steps in the **sinc** function are executed. When debugging a function, it is a good idea to use **printf** statements to provide a memory snapshot of the actual parameters before the function is referenced, and of the formal parameters at the beginning of the function.

Valid references to the **sinc** function can also include expressions and can include other function references, as shown in these example references to the **sinc** function:

```
printf("%f \n",sinc(x+2.5));

scanf("%lf",&y);
printf("%f \n",sinc(y));

z = x*x + sinc(2*x);

w = sinc(fabs(y));
```

In all these example references, the formal parameter is still **x**, but the actual parameter is **x+2.5**, or **y**, or **2*x**, or **fabs(y)**, depending on the reference selected.

If a function has more than one parameter, the formal parameters and the actual parameters must match in number, type, and order. A mismatch between the number of formal parameters and actual parameters can be detected by the compiler using the function prototype statement. If the type of an actual parameter is not the same as the corresponding formal parameter, the value of the actual parameter will be converted to the appropriate type. This conversion is called **coercion of arguments** and may or may not cause errors. Recall that converting values to a higher type (such as from **float** to **double**) generally works correctly; converting values to a lower type (such as from **float** to **int**) often introduces errors.

Coercion of argument

Additional errors can be introduced if the actual parameters are out of order. These errors may not be detected by the compiler and can be difficult to detect. Therefore, be especially careful that the order of the formal parameters and the actual parameters match.

Call-by-value

The function reference in the **sinc** example is a **call-by-value** reference, or a **reference by value**. In general, a C function cannot change the value of an actual parameter. An exception occurs when an actual parameter is an array; this will be discussed in the next chapter.

Practice!

Consider the following function:

```
/*--------------------------------------------------------*/
int positive(double a, double b, double c)
{
   int count = 0;

   if (a >= 0)
      count++;
   if (b >= 0)
      count++;
   if (c >= 0)
      count++;

   return count;
}
/*--------------------------------------------------------*/
```

Assume that the function is referenced with the following statements:

```
x = 25;
total = positive(x, sqrt(x), x-30);
```

1.   Show the memory snapshot of the actual parameters and the formal parameters.
2.   What is the new value of **total**?

STORAGE CLASS AND SCOPE

In the example programs presented thus far, we have declared variables within a **main** function and within programmer-defined functions. It is also valid to define a variable before the **main** function. Therefore, it is important to be able to determine

Scope

the **scope** of a function or a variable, where scope refers to the portion of the program in which it is valid to reference the function or variable. Scope is also sometimes defined in terms of the portion of the program in which the function or variable is visible or accessible. Because the scope of a variable is directly related to its **storage class**, we also discuss three storage classes—automatic, external, and static.

First, we define the difference between local variables and global vari-

Local variables

ables. **Local variables** are defined within a function and include the formal parameters and any other variables declared in the function. A local variable can be accessed only in the function that defined it. A local variable has a value when its function is being executed, but its value is not retained when the func-

Global variables

tion is completed. **Global variables** are defined outside the **main** function and other programmer-defined functions so they can be accessed by any function within the program. However, to reference a global or an external variable, a declaration within the function must include the keyword **extern** before the type designation to tell the computer to look outside the function for the variable. The **automatic storage class** is used to represent local variables. This is the default storage class, but it can also be specified with the keyword **auto** before the type designation. The **external storage class** is used to represent global variables; the **extern** designation must be used within functions; it is optional in the original definition of a global variable.

Style

The memory assigned to an external variable is retained for the duration of the program. Although an external variable can be referenced from a function using the proper declaration, using global variables is generally discouraged. *In general, parameters are preferred for transferring information to a function because the parameter is evident in the function prototype, whereas the external variable is not visible in the function prototype.*

Function names also have external storage class and can be referenced from other functions. Function prototypes included outside of any function are also external references and are available to all other functions in the program. This explains why we do not need to include **math.h** in every function that references a mathematical function. However, the parameter variables in the function prototype are known only in the function prototype statement.

The **static** storage class is used to specify that the memory for a variable should be retained during the entire program execution. Therefore, if a local variable in a function is given a **static storage class** assignment by using the keyword `static` before its type specification, the variable will not lose its value when the program exits the function in which it is defined. A `static` variable could be used to count the number of times that a function was invoked because the value of the count would be preserved from one function call to another.

CHAPTER SUMMARY

Most programs in C benefit from using both library and programmer-defined functions. Functions allow us to reuse software and to employ abstraction in our solution, and, hence, reduce development time and increase the quality of the software.

KEY TERMS

abstraction

actual parameter

automatic class

call by value

coercion of arguments

driver

external class

formal parameter

function prototype

global variable

invoke

library function

local variable

modularity

module

programmer-defined function

reusability

static class

scope

void function

C STATEMENT SUMMARY

Function definition

```
return_type function_name(parameter declarations)
{
   declarations;
   statements;
}
```

Return statement

```
return;
return (a + b)/2;
```

Function Prototype

```
double sinc(double x);
double sinc(double);
void print_data(int x, int y);
```

Style NOTES

1. A program with several modules is easier to read and understand than one long **main** function.
2. Select the name of the function to indicate the purpose of the function.
3. Use a special line, such as a line of dashes, to separate programmer-defined functions from the **main** function and other programmer-defined functions.
4. Use a consistent order for functions, such as the **main** function first, followed by additional functions in the order in which they are referenced.
5. Use parameter identifiers in prototype statements to help document the order and definition of the parameters.
6. List the function prototypes on separate lines so that they are easy to identify.
7. Use the parameter list instead of external variables to transmit information to a function.

DEBUGGING NOTES

1. If you are having difficulty understanding the error messages from a compiler, try running the program on another compiler to obtain different error messages.
2. When debugging a long program, add comment indicators (**/*** and ***/**) around some sections of the code so that you can focus on other parts of the program.
3. Test a complicated function by itself, using a driver program.
4. Make sure that the value returned from a function matches the function return_type. If necessary, use the cast operator to convert a value to the proper type.
5. Functions can be defined before or after the **main** function, but not within it.
6. Always use function prototype statements to avoid errors in parameter passing.

7. Use `printf` statements to generate memory snapshots of the actual parameters before a function is referenced and of the formal parameters at the beginning of the function.

8. Carefully match the type, order, and number of actual parameters with the formal parameters of a function.

PROBLEMS

Print Routines. The following problems develop functions that are useful when printing reports. These are all **void** functions because they print information, but they do not return any values.

1. Write and test a function that will print your name, course title, and homework number in the following format:

```
Joey Smith
Engineering 101
Homework #5
```

Your name and course title should be included within the output statements; the homework number is an input parameter. Assume that the function prototype is

```
void header(int hw_number);
```

2. Write and test a function that prints two totals in the following format:

```
Summary Information
     Total 1    xxxx.xx
     Total 2    xxxx.xx
     Combined Totals     xxxxx.xx
```

Assume that the function prototype is

```
void summary(double total_1, double total_2);
```

3. Write and test a function that prints the following error message:

```
Error occurred in the processing of the data file.
Recheck the data before rerunning this program.
```

Assume that the function prototype is

```
void error(void);
```

4. Write and test a function that prints an error message in the following format:

```
Errors occurred in processing the data file.
xxx values were out of the appropriate range.
```

The number of values out of range is an input parameter to the function. Assume that the function prototype is

```
void error_total(int error_count);
```

5.   Write and test a function that prints an error message that depends on the value in an integer parameter. If the value of the error flag is 1, print

Error identified in the distance data.

If the value of the error flag is 2, print

Error identified in the velocity data.

If the value of the error flag is 3, print

Error identified in the acceleration data.

For all other values of the error flag, print

Unidentified error occurred.

Assume that the function prototype is

```
void error_message(int error_flag);
```

Function Evaluations. Functions are often used to evaluate a mathematical function that is not included in the Standard C library. The following problems develop functions to return function values.

6.   Write and test a function that receives three integers. The function should return the maximum value. Assume that the function prototype is

```
int maximum_int(int a, int b, int c);
```

7.   Write and test a function that returns the value of $f(x)$ where

$$f(x) = \frac{3x^2 + x - 2}{x^2 - 2x + 1}$$

Assume that the function prototype is

```
double f(double x);
```

8.   Write and test a function that returns the value of $g(x)$ where

$$g(x) = 0, \text{ if } x < 0$$

$$= 6e^{(x - 3)}, \text{ if } x \geq 0$$

Assume that the function prototype is

```
double g(double x);
```

9. Write and test a function that returns the radius of the line from a point (x,y) on a plane to the origin, where

$$radius = \sqrt{x^2 + y^2}$$

Assume that the function prototype is

```
double radius (double x, double y);
```

10. Write and test a function that returns the quadrant number of a point (x,y) on a plane. Recall that points in quadrant 1 have positive x and y values, points in quadrant 2 have a negative x value and a positive y value, points in quadrant 3 have negative x and y values, and the remaining points are in quadrant 4. If a point is on an axis, choose the quadrant with the lower quadrant number. Assume that the function prototype is

```
int quadrant(double x, double y);
```

5

Courtesy of United Airlines.

GRAND CHALLENGE:
Speech Recognition

The modern jet cockpit has literally hundreds of switches and gauges. Several research programs are investigating the feasibility of using a speech-recognition system in the cockpit to serve as a pilot's assistant. The system would respond to verbal requests from the pilot for information such as fuel status or altitude. The pilot would use words from a small vocabulary that the computer had been trained to understand. In addition to understanding a specific vocabulary, the system would also have to be trained using the speech for the pilot who would be using the system. This training information could be stored on a diskette and inserted into the onboard computer at the beginning of a flight so the system could recognize the current pilot. The computer system would also use speech synthesis to respond to the pilot's request for information.

One-Dimensional Arrays

OBJECTIVES

This chapter introduces the **array,** a data structure used frequently in solving engineering problems. One-dimensional arrays are discussed in detail, with examples that illustrate defining and initializing arrays, perform computations with arrays, use arrays in input and output statements, and use arrays as function arguments. A set of functions for performing simple statistical measurements on one-dimensional arrays is also developed.

5.1   Array Definitions and Computations

When solving engineering problems, it is important to be able to visualize the data related to the problem. Sometimes the data is just a single number, such as the radius of a circle. Other times the data may be coordinates in a plane that can be represented as a pair of numbers, with one number representing the x-coordinate and the other number representing the y-coordinate. There are also times when we want to work with a set of similar data values, but we do not want to give each value a separate name. For example, suppose that we have a set of 100 temperature measurements that we want to use to perform several computations. Obviously, we do not want to use 100 different names for the temperature measurements, so we need a method for working with a group of values using a single identifier. One solution to this problem uses a data structure called an array. A **one-dimensional**

One-dimensional
array

array can be visualized as a list of values arranged in either a row or a column, as shown below:

5	0	−1	2	15	2
s[0]	s[1]	s[2]	s[3]	s[4]	s[5]

t[0]	0.0
t[1]	0.1
t[2]	0.2
t[3]	0.3

Subscript

We assign an identifier to an array, and then distinguish between **elements** or values in the array using **subscripts**. In C, the subscripts always start with 0 and increment by 1. Thus, using the example arrays, the first value in the **s** array is referenced by **s[0]**, and the third value in the **t** array is referenced by **t[2]**.

Arrays are convenient for storing and handling large amounts of data, so there is a tendency to use them in algorithms when they are not necessary. Arrays are more complicated to use than simple variables and make programs longer and more difficult to debug. Therefore, use arrays only when it is necessary to have the complete set of data available in memory.

DEFINITION AND INITIALIZATION

An array is defined using declaration statements. An integer expression in brackets follows the identifier and specifies the number of elements in the array. Note that all elements in an array must be the same data type. The declaration statements for the two example arrays are as follows:

```
int s[6];
double t[4];
```

An array can be initialized with declaration statements or with program statements. To initialize the array with the declaration statement, the values are specified in a sequence that is separated by commas and enclosed in braces. The following statements define and initialize the example arrays **s** and **t**:

```
int s[6]={5, 0, -1, 2, 15, 2};
double t[4]={0.0, 0.1, 0.2, 0.3};
```

If the initializing sequence is shorter than the array, the rest of the values are initialized to zero. Hence, the following statement defines an integer array of 100 values; each value is also initialized to zero:

```
int s[100]={0};
```

If an array is specified without a size but with an initialization sequence, the size is defined to be equal to the number of value in the sequence. Thus, the following statements also define the arrays **s** and **t**:

```
int s[]={5, 0, -1, 2, 15, 2};
double t[]={0.0, 0.1, 0.2, 0.3};
```

The size of an array must be specified in the declaration statement, using either a constant within brackets or by an initialization sequence within braces.

Arrays can also be initialized with program statements. For example, suppose that we want to fill a **double** array **g** with the values 0.0, 0.5, 1.0, 1.5, ... , 10.0. Because there are 21 values, listing the values on the declaration statement would be tedious. Thus, we use the following statements to define and initialize this array:

```
/*  Declare variables.   */
int k;
double g[21];
...
/*  Initialize the array g.   */
for (k=0; k<=20; k++)
   g[k] = k*0.5;
```

It is important to recognize that the condition in this **for** statement must specify a final subscript value of 20, and not 21. It is a common mistake to specify a subscript that is one value more than the largest valid subscript. This error can be very difficult to find because it accesses values outside the array. Because this error is generally not detected during the program execution, it is important to be careful about exceeding the array subscripts. In our programs, we select conditions in **for** loops that specifically use the final value as a reminder to ourselves to carefully write the condition to avoid errors. Thus, in this example, we use the condition **k<=20** instead of **k<21**, although both work properly. *Also, we will generally use k as the subscript for a one-dimensional array.*

Style

Arrays are often used to store information that is read from data files. For example, suppose that we have a data file named **sensor3.dat** that contains ten time and motion measurements collected from a seismometer. To read these values into arrays named **time** and **motion**, we could use these statements:

```
/*  Declare variables.  */
int k;
double time[10], motion[10];
FILE *sensor3;
...
/*  Open file and read data into arrays.  */
sensor3 = fopen("sensor3.dat","r");
for (k=0; k<=9; k++)
   fscanf(sensor3,"%lf %lf",&time[k],&motion[k]);
```

Practice!

Show the contents of the arrays defined in each of the following sets of statements.

1. `int x[10]={-5, 4, 3};`

-5	4	3	0	0	0	0	0	0	0

2.  ```
    double z[4];
    ...
    z[1] = -5.5;
    z[2] = z[3] = fabs(z[1]);
    ```

3.  ```
    int k, time[9];
    ...
    for (k=0; k<=8; k++)
       time[k] = (k-4)*0.1;
    ```

-0.4	-0.3	-0.2	-0.1	0	0.1	0.2	0.3	0.4

COMPUTATIONS AND I/O

Computations with array elements are specified just like computations with simple variables, but a subscript must be used to specify an individual array element. To illustrate, the following program reads an array **y** of 100 floating-point values from a data file. The program determines the average value of the array and stores it in **y_ave**. Then, the number of values in the array **y** that are greater than the average are counted and printed.

```
/*-------------------------------------------------------*/
/*  Program chapter5_1                                   */
/*                                                       */
/*  This program reads 100 values from a data file       */
/*  and determines the number of values greater          */
/*  than the average.                                    */

#include <stdio.h>
#include <stdlib.h>
#define FILENAME "lab.dat"
```

```
main()
{
   /*  Declare and initialize variables.   */
   int k, count=0;
   double y[100], y_ave, sum=0;
   FILE *lab;

   /*  Open file, read data into an array,  */
   /*  and compute a sum of the values.      */
   lab = fopen(FILENAME,"r");
   for (k=0; k<=99; k++)
   {
      fscanf(lab,"%lf",&y[k]);
      sum += y[k];
   }

   /*  Compute average and count values that  */
   /*  are greater than the average.          */
   y_ave = sum/100;
   for (k=0; k<=99; k++)
      if (y[k] > y_ave)
         count++;

   /*  Print count.  */
   printf("%i values greater than the average \n",count);

   /*  Close file and exit program.  */
   fclose(lab);
   return EXIT_SUCCESS;
}
/*-------------------------------------------------------*/
```

If the purpose of this program had been to determine the average of the values in the data file, an array would not have been necessary. The loop to read values could read each value into the same variable, adding its value to a sum before the next value is read. However, because we needed to compare each value to the average in order to count the number of values greater than the average, an array was needed so that we could access each value again.

Array values are printed using a subscript to specify the individual value desired. For example, the following statement prints the first and last values of the array y used in the previous example:

```
printf("first and last array values: \n");
printf("%f %f \n",y[0],y[99]);
```

The following loop prints all 100 values of y, one per line:

```
printf("y values: \n");
for (k=0; k<=99; k++)
   printf("%f \n",y[k]);
```

When printing a large array, such as this one, we probably would like to print several numbers on the same line. The following statements use the modulus operator to skip to a new line before each group of five values is printed:

```
printf("y values: \n");
for (k=0; k<=99; k++)
   if (k%5 == 0)
      printf("\n %f ",y[k]);
   else
      printf("%f ",y[k]);
printf("\n");
```

Statements similar to the ones illustrated here can also be used to write array values to a data file. For example, the following statement will print the value of y[k] on a line in a data file with a file pointer **sensor**:

```
fprintf(sensor,"%f \n",y[k]);
```

The new line indicator is included, so the next value written to the file will be on a new line.

The number of elements in an array is used in the array declaration and in loops used to access the elements in the array. If the number of elements is changed, there are several places in the program that need to be modified. *Changing the size of an array is simplified if a symbolic constant is used to specify the size of the array.* Then, to change the size, only the preprocessor directive needs to be changed. This style suggestion is especially important in programs that contain many modules or in programming environments in which several programmers are working on the same software project.

Style

Table 5.1 gives an updated precedence order that includes subscript brackets. Brackets and parentheses are associated before the other operators. If parentheses and brackets are nested, the innermost set is evaluated first.

TABLE 5.1 Operator Precedence		
Precedence	Operation	Associativity
1	( ) [ ]	innermost first
2	+ - ++ -- (type) !	right to left
3	* / %	left to right
4	+ -	left to right
5	< <= > >=	left to right
6	== !=	left to right
7	&&	left to right
8	||	left to right
9	= += -= *= /= %=	right to left

Practice!

Assume that the variable **k** and the array **s** have been defined with the following statement:

```
int k, s[]={3, 8, 15, 21, 30, 41};
```

Give the output for each of the following sets of statements.

1.  ```
    for (k=0; k<=5; k+=2)
        printf("%i %i \n",s[k], s[k+1]);
    ```
    3 8
    15 21
    30 41

2.  ```
    for (k=0; k<=5; k++)
        if (s[k]%2 == 0)
            printf("%i ",s[k]);
    ```
    8 30

5.2   Arrays as Function Arguments

When the information in an array is passed to a function, two parameters are usually used; one parameter specifies the specific array, and the other parameter specifies the number of elements used in the array. By specifying the number of elements of the array that are to be used, the function becomes more flexible. For example, if the function specifies an integer array, the function can be used with any integer array. The parameter that specifies the number of elements assures that we use the correct size. Also, the number of elements used in an array may vary from one time to another. For example, the array may use elements read from a data file. The number of elements then depends on the specific data file used when the program is run. In all of these examples, though, the array must be declared to a maximum size in the **main** function. Then the actual number of elements used can be less than or equal to that maximum size.

Consider the following program that reads an array from a data file and then references a function to determine the maximum value in the array. The variable **npts** is used to specify the number of values in the array. The value of **npts** can be less than or equal to the defined size of the array, which is 100. The function has two arguments—the name of the array and the number of points in the array, as indicated in the function prototype statement.

```
/*----------------------------------------------------------*/
/*  Program chapter5_2                                      */
/*                                                          */
/*  This program reads values from a data file and          */
/*  determines the maximum value with a function.           */
```

```c
#include <stdio.h>
#include <stdlib.h>
#define N 100
#define FILENAME "lab.dat"

main()
{
    /*  Declare variables and function prototypes.  */
    int k=0, npts;
    double y[N];
    FILE *lab;
    double array_max(double x[], int n);

    /*  Open file and read data into an array, */
    lab = fopen(FILENAME,"r");
    while (fscanf(lab,"%lf",&y[k]) == 1)
        k++;
    npts = k;

    /*  Find and print the maximum value.  */
    printf("Maximum value: %f \n",array_max(y,npts));

    /*  Close file and exit program.  */
    fclose(lab);
    return EXIT_SUCCESS;
}
/*-------------------------------------------------------*/
/*   This function returns the maximum                   */
/*   value in the array x with n elements.               */

double array_max(double x[], int n)
{
    /*  Declare variables.  */
    int k;
    double max_x;

    /*  Determine maximum value in the array.  */
    max_x = x[0];
    for (k=1; k<=n-1; k++)
        if (x[k] > max_x)
            max_x = x[k];

    /*  Return maximum value.  */
    return max_x;
}
/*-------------------------------------------------------*/
```

This program assumes that there will not be more than 100 values in the file; otherwise, this program will not work correctly. Arrays must be specified to be as large as, or larger than, the maximum number of values to be read into them.

The purpose of program **chapter5_2** was to illustrate the use of an array as a function argument. If the purpose of this program had been to determine the maximum of the data values in the file, an array would not have been necessary; the maximum could have been determined as the data values were read.

CALL-BY-ADDRESS REFERENCES

There is a very significant difference in using arrays as parameters and in using simple variables as parameters. When a simple variable is used as a parameter, the value is passed to the formal parameter in the function, and the value of the original value cannot be changed; this is a call-by-value reference. When an array is used as a parameter, the memory address of the array is passed to the function instead of the entire set of values in the array. Therefore, the function references values in the original array; this is a **call-by-address** reference. Because a function accesses the original array values, we must be very careful that we do not inadvertently change values in an array within a function. Of course, there may also be occasions when we wish to change the values in the array.

Call-by-address

Practice!

Assume that the following variables are defined:

```
int k=6;
double data[]={1.5, 3.2, -6.1, 9.8, 8.7, 5.2};
```

Give the values of the following expressions that reference the **array_max** function presented in this section.

1.   **array_max(data,6);** 9.8
2.   **array_max(data,5);** 9.8
3.   **array_max(data,k-3);** 3.2
4.   **array_max(data,k%5);** 1.5

STATISTICAL MEASUREMENTS

Analyzing data collected from engineering experiments is an important part of evaluating the experiments. This analysis ranges from simple computations on the data, such as calculating the average value, to more complicated analyses. Many of the computations or measurements using data are statistical measurements because they have statistical properties that change from one set of data to another. For example, the sine of 60° is an exact value that is the same value every time we compute it, but the number of miles to the gallon that we get with our car is a statistical measurement because it varies somewhat depending on parameters such as the temperature, the speed that we travel, the type of road, and whether we are in the mountains or the desert.

When evaluating a set of experimental data, we often compute the maximum value, minimum value, mean or average value, and the median. In this section we develop functions that can be used to compute these values using an array as input. These functions will be useful in solutions to problems at the end of the chapter. It is important to note that these functions assume that there is at least one value in the array.

Maximum, Minimum. A function for determining the maximum value in an array was presented earlier in this section; a similar function can easily be developed for determining the minimum value.

Mean value

Average. The Greek symbol μ (mu) is used to represent the average or **mean value**, as shown in the following equation, which uses summation notation:

$$\mu = \frac{\sum_{k=0}^{n-1} x_k}{n} \qquad\qquad 5.1$$

where $\sum_{k=0}^{n-1} x_k = x_0 + x_1 + x_2 + \ldots + x_{n-1}$. The average of a set of values is always a floating-point value, even if all the data values are integers. This function computes the mean value of a **double** array of **n** values:

```
/*-----------------------------------------------------*/
/*   This function returns the average or              */
/*   mean value of an array with n elements.           */

double array_mean(double x[], int n)
{
   /*  Declare and initialize variables.  */
   int k;
   double sum=0;

   /*  Determine mean value.  */
   for (k=0; k<=n-1; k++)
      sum += x[k];

   /*  Return mean value.  */
   return sum/n;
}
/*-----------------------------------------------------*/
```

Note that the variable **sum** was initialized to zero on the declaration statement. It could also have been initialized to zero with an assignment statement. In either case, the value of **sum** is initialized to zero each time that the function is referenced.

Median

Median. The **median** is the value in the middle of a group of values, assuming that the values are sorted. If there is an odd number of values, the median is the value in the middle; if there is an even number of values, the median is the average of the values in the two middle positions. For example, the median of the values {1, 6, 18, 39, 86} is the middle value, or 18; the median of the values {1, 6, 18, 39, 86, 91} is the average of the two middle values, or (18 + 39)/2 or 28.5. Assume that a group of sorted values is stored in an array and that **n** contains the number of values in the array. If **n** is odd, the subscript of the middle value can be represented by **floor(n/2)**, as in **floor(5/2)**, which is 2. If **n** is even, then the subscripts of the two middle values can be represented by **floor(n/2)-1** and **floor(n/2)**, as in **floor(6/2)-1** and **floor(6/2)**, which are 2 and 3 in the example above. The following function determines the median of a set of values stored in an array. We assume that the values are sorted (into either ascending or descending order).

```
/*------------------------------------------------------*/
/*  This function returns the median                    */
/*  value in an array x with n elements                 */

double array_median(double x[], int n)
{
   /*  Declare variables.  */
   int k;
   double median_x;

   /*  Determine median value. */
   k = floor(n/2);
   if (n%2 != 0)
      median_x = x[k];
   else
      median_x = (x[k-1] + x[k])/2;

   /*  Return median value.  */
   return median_x;
}
/*------------------------------------------------------*/
```

Go through this function by hand using the two sets of data values given in this discussion.

CHAPTER SUMMARY

An array is a data structure often used to store engineering data that are best represented by a list of information. Examples were developed in this chapter to illustrate array definitions, array initializations, computations with arrays, input and output with arrays, and arrays as function parameters. A set of simple statistical functions was developed for computing statistical information for analyzing one-dimensional arrays.

KEY TERMS

array

call-by-address

element

mean value

median

one-dimensional array

subscript

C STATEMENT SUMMARY

Array Declaration

```
int a[5], b[]={2, 3, -1};
```

Style NOTES

1. The variable **k** is commonly used as a subscript for a one-dimensional array.
2. Use symbolic constants to declare the size of an array so that it is easy to modify.

DEBUGGING NOTES

1. Use arrays only when it is necessary to keep all the data available in memory.
2. Be careful not to exceed the maximum subscript value when referencing an element in an array.
3. Select conditions in **for** loops to specifically use an equality with the maximum subscript value; this helps avoid errors with subscript ranges.
4. An array must be declared to be as large as, or larger than, the maximum number of values to be stored in it.
5. Because an array reference in a function is a call-by-address reference, be careful that you do not inadvertently change values in an array in the function.

PROBLEMS

The following problems are all stated in terms of writing a function that has an array as an argument. Alternative problems can be defined that do not require functions by changing each problem to one of reading 20 values from the keyboard and storing them in an array. The program should then determine and print the value computed as an array characteristic (problems 1–5) or modify and print the array values (problems 6–10).

Array Characteristics. It is very convenient to have a group of functions for determining information stored in an array. The function array_max, array_mean, and array_median developed in this chapter are examples of these types of routines. The following problems develop additional functions that are useful for working with arrays.

1. Write and test a function that will determine if the values in an array are in ascending order or descending order. The function value should be 1 if the array values are in ascending order, –1 if they are in descending order, and 0 if they are in neither order. Assume that the function prototype is the following:

    ```
    int order(int x[], int npts);
    ```

2. Write and test a function that will compare values in two arrays of the same size. If the values in the two arrays are the same, the function should return a 1; otherwise, it should return 0. Assume that the function prototype is the following:

    ```
    int identical(int a[], int b[], int npts);
    ```

3. Write and test a function that counts the number of values in an array that are greater than a specified target value. Assume that the function prototype is the following:

    ```
    int greater_count(int x[], int npts, int target);
    ```

4. Write and test a function that counts the number of values in an array that are less than or equal to a specified target value. Use the function developed in problem 3 in your solution. Assume that the function prototype is the following:

    ```
    int less_equal_count(int x[], int npts, int target);
    ```

5. Write and test a function that determines the largest difference between two adjacent values in an array. If there is only one value in the array, the difference should be zero. Assume that the function prototype is the following:

    ```
    double diff(double y[], int npts);
    ```

Array Modification. The following set of functions modifies the values in an array.

6.   Assume that an array contains angles in radians. Write a function that converts the angles to degrees. Assume that the function prototype is the following:

```
void rad_to_deg(double b[], int npts);
```

7.   Assume that an array contains angles in degrees. Write a function that converts any angles outside of the interval [0,360] to an equivalent angle in the interval [0,360]. For example, an angle of 380.5 degrees should be converted to 20.5 degrees. Assume that the function prototype is the following:

```
void reduce_angle(double b[], int npts);
```

8.   Write and test a function that will replace (or "clip") any value above a specified value with the specified value. Assume that the function prototype is the following:

```
void clip(double b[], int npts, double peak_value);
```

To illustrate, the following function reference will replace any value above 5.0 in the array **x** with the value 5.0:

```
clip(x, n, 5.0);
```

9.   Write and test a function that will subtract the mean value of an array from each element in the array. (The mean value of these new values is then always zero.) Use the function **array_mean** in your function. Assume that the function prototype is the following:

```
void remove_mean(double x[], int npts);
```

10.   There are a number of ways to normalize, or scale, a set of values. One common normalization technique scales the values so that the minimum value goes to 0, the maximum value goes to 1, and other values are scaled accordingly. Using this normalization, the values in the array below are normalized:

Array values:

-2	-1	2	0

Normalized array values:

0.0	0.25	1.0	0.5

The equation that computes the normalized value from a value x_k in the array is the following:

$$\text{Normalized } x_k = \frac{x_k - min_x}{max_x - min_x}$$

where min_x and max_x represent the minimum and maximum values in the array x. If you substitute the minimum value for x_k in this equation, the numerator is zero; thus, the normalized value for the minimum is zero. If you substitute the maximum value for x_k in this equation, the numerator and denominator are the same value; hence, the normalized value for the maximum is 1.0. Write and test a function that has a one-dimensional **double** array and the number of values in the array as its arguments. Normalize the values in the array using the technique presented above. Use the function **array_max** that was developed in this chapter. Assume that the function prototype is the following:

```
void norm(double x[], int npts);
```

5

6

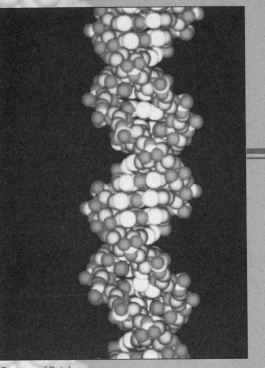

Courtesy of Rainbow.

GRAND CHALLENGE:
Mapping the Human Genome

The deciphering of the human genetic code involves locating, identifying, and determining the function of each of the 50,000 to 100,000 genes that are contained in human DNA. Each gene is a double-helix strand composed of base pairs of adenine bonded with thymine, or cytosine bonded with guanine, that are arranged in a steplike manner with phosphate groups along the side. DNA directs the production of proteins, so the proteins produced by a cell provide a key to the sequence of base pairs in the DNA. Instrumentation developed for genetic engineering is extremely useful in this detective work. A protein sequencer developed in 1969 can identify the sequence of amino acids in a protein molecule. Once the amino acid order is known, biologists can begin to identify the gene that made the protein. A DNA synthesizer, developed in 1982, can build small genes or gene fragments out of DNA. This research and its associated instrumentation are key components in beginning to address the mapping of the human genome.

Character Data

OBJECTIVES

Character information is an important type of information to represent and to manipulate in engineering problem solutions. Each character is stored using a binary code. The ASCII code is the most commonly used code, and it is discussed in detail in this chapter. Examples are presented to demonstrate that character information can be processed as character data types or as integers that correspond to the ASCII code values. The initialization of character variables is discussed, and new I/O statements are presented for reading and printing characters. A number of functions from the Standard C library that work with characters are presented, and functions are developed that use characters as arguments.

6.1   Character Information

Numeric information is represented in a C program as integers or floating-point values. These numeric values can be single, independent values or they can be grouped together in an array. Numeric values are often used in arithmetic computations. In many problem solutions, we also need to store and manipulate nonnumeric information, which may consist of alphabetic characters, digits, and special characters. Even though nonnumeric information can contain digits, these digits are not values generally used in arithmetic computations; instead, they are digits in an address, a phone number, or a social security number.

Recall that all information stored in a computer is represented internally as sequences of binary digits (0 or 1). In general, we do not need to be concerned about this binary representation because the compiler and the computer perform the necessary steps to convert our programs to binary and then to execute them. However, in order to work with **characters,** we need to understand more about their representation in the **computer's** memory. Each character corresponds to a **binary code** value. The most commonly used binary codes are

ASCII

ASCII (American Standard Code for Information Interchange) and **EBCDIC** (Extended Binary Coded Decimal Interchange Code). In the discussions that follow, we assume that ASCII code is used to represent characters. Table 6.1 contains a few characters, their binary form in ASCII, and the integer values that correspond to the binary values. Thus, the character a is represented by the binary value 1100001, which is equivalent to an integer value of 97. A total of 128 characters can be represented in the ASCII code; a complete ASCII code table is given in Appendix A.

Once a character is stored in memory as a binary value, the binary value can be interpreted as a character or as an integer, as illustrated in Table 6.1. Thus, when we define variables that are to be used for storing characters, we can define them as either characters or integers. However, it is important to note that the binary representation for a character digit is not equal to the binary representation for an integer digit. From Table 6.1 we see that the binary representation of the digit 3 is equivalent to the binary representation of the integer 51.

TABLE 6.1 Examples of ASCII Codes		
Character	ASCII Code	Integer Equivalent
newline, \n	0001010	10
%	0100101	37
3	0110011	51
A	1000001	65
a	1100001	97
b	1100010	98
c	1100011	99

Thus, performing a computation with the character representation of a digit does not yield the same result as performing the computation with the integer representation of the digit.

Nonnumeric information can be represented by constants or by variables in our programs. A character constant is enclosed in single quotes, as in **'A'**, **'b'**, and **'3'**. A variable that is going to contain a character can be defined as an integer or as a character data type **(char)**. Integer arrays can be used to represent a group of characters. C also allows the definition of a character string, but character strings are not discussed in this text.

Practice!

Give integer values for the following characters using the ASCII code table from Appendix A.

1. **(**   2. **<**
3. **G**   4. **g**

Give the characters (or meaning) that correspond to each of the following binary code values.

5. 1001111   6. 0100100
7. 1110101   8. 1011110

6.2 Character Initialization and Computations

The binary representation for a character can be interpreted as a character or as an integer. Similarly, the value of a small positive integer can be printed as a character or an integer, and the value of a character variable (defined using the **char** type) can be printed as a character or an integer. To print a value as an integer, the **%i** or **%d** specifier is used; to print a value as a character, the **%c** specifier is used. The following statements illustrate printing the same value as an integer and as a character:

```
/*  Declare and initialize variables.  */
int k=97;
char c='a';
...
/*  Print both values as characters.  */
printf("value of k: %c; value of c: %c \n",k,c);
/*  Print both values as integers.  */
printf("value of k: %i; value of c: %i \n",k,c);
```

The output of these statements is

```
value of k: a; value of c: a
value of k: 97; value of c: 97
```

In many problem solutions, either type of variable can be used to store and manipulate a character. However, there are situations in which a character should be stored in an integer variable, as illustrated in the following discussion on character I/O.

CHARACTER I/O

Although the **printf** and **scanf** functions can be used to read characters using the **%c** specifier, C also contains special functions for reading and printing characters. The **getchar** function reads a character from the keyboard and returns the integer value of the character; the **putchar** function prints a character to the computer screen, and then also returns the same character. The prototype statements for these functions are

```
int putchar(int);
int getchar(void);
```

Text stream

EOF

Both functions use a **text stream,** which is composed of a sequence of characters. For the **getchar** function, the text stream is the line entered through the keyboard; for the **putchar** function, the text stream is the line printed on the screen. In either case, the text stream can be separated into lines by newline characters. The end of a text stream is indicated with a special value, **EOF**. This special value, **EOF**, is a symbolic constant defined in **stdio.h**.

The execution of the **putchar** function causes the character that corresponds to the integer argument to be written to the computer screen. If several **putchar** function references are made in a row, the characters are printed one after another on the same line, until a newline character is printed. Thus, the following statements cause the characters **ab** to be printed on one line, followed by **c** on the next line:

```
putchar('a');
putchar('b');
putchar('\n');
putchar('c');
```

The same information could be printed using the integer values that correspond to the characters (see Table 6.1 on page 136):

```
putchar(97);
putchar(98);
putchar(10);
putchar(99);
```

In general, we prefer to use character constants instead of their binary equivalents in order to make the program easier to read.

When a **getchar** function is executed, the next character in the current input text stream is obtained and returned as the function value. If there is no current text stream, a line of information is obtained from the keyboard. This line must be ended by pressing the return key, which corresponds to entering a newline character. Thus, when the first **getchar** function is executed in a program, a line of information is read from the keyboard, but only the first character in the line is returned by the function. When the next **getchar** function reference is executed, the second character from the line is returned by the function. Successive references continue to return additional characters, until the character returned is a newline character; this signifies that we have reached the end of the current line. Then, the next reference to the **getchar** function causes a new line of information to be read from the keyboard into the text stream. This processing of the text stream by lines continues until the **EOF** character is entered through the keyboard.

A variable defined with the **char** data type can represent only the 128 ASCII characters, but a variable read by the **getchar** function must be able to represent all 128 ASCII characters plus the value representing **EOF**. Because an integer variable can represent more than 128 values, we use an **int** type instead of a **char** type for a variable read by the **getchar** function so that we can also detect the end of the text stream.

The value of the **EOF** character is system dependent; in the Borland Turbo C++ environment, the **EOF** character is entered by pressing the control (ctrl) key, and then pressing the **z** key while the control key is still pressed. This combination of characters is often written as ^z, but this is not the same as pressing the ^ key with the **z** key. In the Borland Turbo C++ environment, this **EOF** character is represented by the integer value −1. (Note that you cannot enter −1 for the **EOF** character because it will be interpreted as a minus sign followed by the digit 1.) To determine the integer value of the **EOF** character on your system, execute the following statement:

```
printf("EOF = %i \n",EOF);
```

The sequence of characters that represents the **EOF** character on many UNIX systems is ^d. To determine the sequence of characters that represents the **EOF** character on other systems, consult your instructor or a computing center consultant.

To illustrate the use of the **getchar** and **putchar** functions, consider the following program that reads characters from the keyboard and prints them to the screen. It also computes and prints a count of the characters read, including spaces and newline characters, but not including the **EOF** character. Note that the user is reminded of the sequence necessary to terminate the text stream.

```
/*-------------------------------------------------------*/
/*   Program chapter6_1                                  */
/*                                                       */
/*   This program demonstrates the relationship          */
/*   between a text stream and character I/O by          */
/*   reading characters from the keyboard and then       */
/*   printing them to the screen.                        */

#include <stdio.h>
#include <stdlib.h>

main()
{
   /*  Declare and initialize variables.  */
   int c, count=0;

   /*  Read, print, and count characters.  */
   printf("Enter characters (^z to quit): \n");
   c = getchar();
   count++;
   while (c != EOF)
   {
      putchar(c);
      c = getchar();
      count++;
   }

   /*  Print the number of characters printed.  */
   printf("%i characters printed. \n",count-1);

   /*  Exit program.  */
   return EXIT_SUCCESS;
}
/*-------------------------------------------------------*/
```

When the first **getchar** function is executed, a line of text is obtained from the keyboard. (Note that this line of text must be ended by pressing the return key, which is equivalent to a newline character.) The first reference to the **getchar** function returns the value of the first character of the line in the variable **c**, but successive executions of the **getchar** function cause additional characters on the line to be read. Therefore, you may enter as many characters as you want on a line, but processing of the program will not continue until you press the return (or enter) key.

An example of the information displayed on the screen during a sample execution of this program is the following:

```
Enter characters (^z to quit):
abcd
abcd
z
z
1w2e3r $
1w2e3r $
^Z
16 characters printed.
```

The first line of characters was **abcd** followed by a newline, the second line contained the character **z** followed by a newline, and the third line contained the characters **1w2e3r $** followed by a newline. The fourth line contained the **EOF** representation followed by a newline; the **EOF** representation caused the program to be terminated. Thus, a total of $5 + 2 + 9 + 1$, or 17 characters, was read, but only 16 were printed.

An interesting variation of program **chapter6_1** is shown in the next program, which prints each character twice and also counts the number of lines read. Note that each character is read within the evaluation of the condition for the **while** loop:

```
while ((c = getchar()) != EOF)
```

Because the value of the statement

```
c = getchar();
```

is equal to **c**, this is equivalent to referencing the **getchar** function to obtain a value for **c** and then comparing the value in **c** to **EOF**. The parentheses around the statement **c = getchar()** are necessary because **!=** has a higher priority than **=**.

```
/*------------------------------------------------------*/
/*  Program chapter6_2                                  */
/*                                                      */
/*  This program reads characters from the keyboard     */
/*  and prints them twice on the screen.  It also       */
/*  counts and prints the number of lines read.         */

#include <stdio.h>
#include <stdlib.h>
#define NEWLINE '\n'

main()
{
    /*  Declare and initialize variables.  */
    int c, count=0;
```

```
      /*  Read and print characters.  */
      printf("Enter characters (^z to quit): \n");
      while ((c = getchar()) != EOF)
      {
         putchar(c);
         putchar(c);
         /*  Count the number of lines.  */
         if (c == NEWLINE)
            count++;
      }

      /*  Print the number of lines read.  */
      printf("%i lines read. \n",count);

      /*  Exit program.  */
      return EXIT_SUCCESS;
}
/*-------------------------------------------------------*/
```

Sample output from this program, using the same input as for the previous program, is

```
Enter characters (^z to quit):
abcd
aabbccdd

z
zz

1w2e3r $
11ww22ee33rr  $$

^Z
3 lines read.
```

Note that the extra line following each line of output is generated by the duplication of the newline character at the end of each input line.

ARRAYS OF CHARACTERS

Because a character can be stored as an integer, groups of characters can be stored in an integer array. Characters in an integer array are accessed using subscripts. Integer arrays containing characters can also be used as function arguments. To illustrate, consider the following program, which counts the number of words in a data file containing text. We assume that words are not split between lines and that there is at least one blank between words. We also assume that the maximum number of characters on a line, including the newline character, is 100. Each character is read using the **fgetc** function; this function reads characters from a text stream in a data file. The argument of the **fgetc** function is a file pointer.

```c
/*-------------------------------------------------------*/
/*   Program chapter6_3                                  */
/*                                                       */
/*   This program reads characters from a data file     */
/*   and counts the number of words line by line.       */

#include <stdio.h>
#include <stdlib.h>
#define FILENAME "text1.dat"
#define NEWLINE '\n'

main()
{
   /*  Declare and initialize variables.  */
   int line[100], k=0, count=0;
   FILE *text1;
   int word_ct(int x[], int npts);

   /*  Open file.  */
   text1 = fopen(FILENAME,"r");

   /*  Read characters and count words.  */
   while ((line[k] = fgetc(text1)) != EOF)
   {
      if (line[k] == NEWLINE)
      {
         if (k != 0)
            count += word_ct(line,k);
         k = 0;
      }
      else
         k++;
   }
   /*  Count words in last line of data.  */
   if (k != 0)
      count += word_ct(line,k);

   /*  Print number of words read.  */
   printf("%i words read. \n",count);

   /*  Exit program.  */
   return EXIT_SUCCESS;
}
/*-------------------------------------------------------*/
/*   This function counts the number of words           */
/*   in an integer array.                               */

int word_ct(int x[], int npts)
{
   /*  Declare and initialize variables.  */
   int count=0, k=0;
```

```
/*  While not at the end of the line,        */
/*  look for the first character of a word. */
while (k <= npts-1)
{
   while (k<=npts-1 && x[k]==' ')
      k++;
   if (k <= npts-1)
      count++;
   while (k<=npts-1 && x[k]!=' ')
      k++;
}

/*  Return word count.  */
return count;
}
/*-------------------------------------------------------*/
```

By using a function to count the number of words in a line, we were able to keep the **main** function short and readable. When the function finds the beginning of a word, it increments the word count. The end of the word is then determined by finding another space or reaching the end of the array. This program was executed with a data file containing the chapter opening discussion on the human genome; the output from the program gave the correct word count of 168.

CHARACTER COMPARISONS

In programs **chapter6_1** and **chapter6_2**, we compared the contents of the integer variable **c** to the **EOF** character; when the binary representations in **c** and **EOF** were equal, the program was terminated. In this comparison, it was clear that the values must be equal in order for the condition to be true. However, suppose **a** and **b** are integer variables that contain characters, and we evaluate the following condition **a < b.** At first it may seem strange to ask if one character is less than another character, but if we consider the comparison in terms of the integer values represented by the characters, then this comparison makes sense. If we want to know if **'?' < 'A'**, we simply need to refer to the ASCII code table in Appendix A. Because the numeric value of **'?'** is 63 and the numeric value of **'A'** is 65, the comparison is true.

Collating
sequence

   The ordering of characters in a specific code, from low to high, is a **collating sequence**. If you study the ASCII collating sequence in Appendix A, some interesting characteristics can be observed. The character codes for the digits 0 through 9 are contiguous, the character codes for the uppercase letters A through Z are contiguous, and the character codes for the lowercase letters a through z are contiguous. Also, digits are less than uppercase letters, which are less than lowercase letters. The difference between an uppercase letter and its corresponding lowercase letter is 32. Finally, special characters are not contiguous; some special characters are before digits, others are after digits, and still others are between uppercase and lowercase letters.
   Consider the following program that counts the number of digits in an input text stream:

```
/*----------------------------------------------------*/
/*  Program chapter6_4                                */
/*                                                    */
/*  This program counts and prints the               */
/*  number of digits in an input text stream.        */

#include <stdio.h>
#include <stdlib.h>

main()
{
    /*  Declare and initialize variables.  */
    int c, count=0;

    /*  Read characters and count digits.  */
    printf("Enter characters (^z to quit): \n");
    while ((c = getchar()) != EOF)
       if ('0'<=c && c<='9')
          ++count;

    /*  Print the number of digits read.  */
    printf("%i digits read. \n",count);

    /*  Exit program.  */
    return EXIT_SUCCESS;
}
/*----------------------------------------------------*/
```

An example interaction with this program is the following:

```
Enter characters (^z to quit):
514 East Sixth St.
Hampton, NH 30255-0345
^Z
12 digits read.
```

An alternative solution to this program is developed in the next section.

6.3   Character Functions

The Standard C library contains a set of functions for use with characters. These functions fall into two categories; one set of functions is used to convert characters between uppercase and lowercase, and the other set is used to perform character comparisons. Each function requires an integer argument, and each function returns an integer value; the prototype statements for these functions are included in the header file ctype.h. The character comparison functions return a nonzero value if the comparison is true; otherwise, they return a zero.

tolower(c)   If c is an uppercase letter, this function returns the corresponding lowercase letter; otherwise, it returns c.

toupper(c)   If c is a lowercase letter, this function returns the corresponding uppercase letter; otherwise, it returns c.

isdigit(c)	This function returns a nonzero value if **c** is a decimal digit; otherwise, it returns a zero.
islower(c)	This function returns a nonzero value if **c** is a lowercase letter; otherwise, it returns a zero.
isupper(c)	This function returns a nonzero value if **c** is an uppercase letter; otherwise, it returns a zero.
isalpha(c)	This function returns a nonzero value if **c** is an uppercase letter or a lowercase letter; otherwise, it returns a zero.
isalnum(c)	This function returns a nonzero value if **c** is an **alphanumeric** character (an alphabetic character or a numeric digit); otherwise, it returns a zero.
iscntrl(c)	This function returns a nonzero value if **c** is a control character; otherwise, it returns a zero. (The **control characters** have integer codes of 0 through 21, and 127.)
isgraph(c)	This function returns a nonzero value if **c** is a character that can be printed, as opposed to a character that cannot be printed, such as a control character or a tab; otherwise, it returns a zero. (The **printing characters** have integer codes from 32 through 126.)
isprint(c)	This function returns a nonzero value if **c** is a printing character (includes a space); otherwise, it returns a zero.
ispunct(c)	This function returns a nonzero value if **c** is a printing character, with the exception of a space or a letter or a digit; otherwise, it returns a zero.
isspace(c)	This function returns a nonzero value if **c** is a space, formfeed, newline, carriage return, horizontal tab, or vertical tab (these characters are also referred to as **white space**); otherwise, the function returns a zero.
isxdigit(c)	This function returns a nonzero value if **c** is a hexadecimal digit, which is a decimal digit or an alphabetic character A through F (or a through f); otherwise, it returns a zero.

Style

These functions perform operations similar to some of the operations that we included in previous programs. *In general, use a library function when possible instead of writing your own statements,* Using library functions also reduces debugging time.

We now rewrite program **chapter6_4** so that it uses a library character function to determine the number of digits in an input text stream. Also, note that an additional **include** statement is needed:

```
/*------------------------------------------------
/*   Program chapter6_5
/*
/*   This program counts and prints the
/*   number of digits in an input text stream.

#include <stdio.h>
#include <stdlib.h>
#include <ctype.h>

main()
{
   /*  Declare and initialize variables.  */
   int c, count=0;

   /*  Read characters and count digits.  */
   printf("Enter characters (^z to quit): \n");
   while ((c = getchar()) != EOF)
      if (isdigit(c))
         ++count;

   /*  Print the number of digits read.  */
   printf("%i digits read. \n",count);

   /*  Exit program.  */
   return EXIT_SUCCESS;
}
/*------------------------------------------------*/
```

The sample output with this program is same as with program **chapter6_4**.

CHAPTER SUMMARY

Using the ASCII binary code to represent characters, we presented techniques for initializing, manipulating, and printing character information. The variables containing the character information were defined as integers and then referenced as either integers or characters, depending on the problem to be solved. Examples were presented that used character information as function arguments.

KEY TERMS

alphanumeric character
ASCII code
binary code
character
collating sequence

control character
EBCDIC code
EOF character
text stream
white space

6

C STATEMENT SUMMARY

Include character function header file

```
#include <ctype.h>
```

Declare and initialize character variable

```
char c = '*';
```

Read character from the keyboard

```
c = getchar();
```

Print character to the screen

```
putchar(c);
```

Style NOTES

1. Use character constants instead of their binary equivalents in program statements.
2. Use character library functions instead of writing similar ones yourself.

DEBUGGING NOTES

1. Remember that the integer representation for a character digit is not the same as the integer representation for the numerical digit.
2. Store the value read by the `getchar` function in an integer variable so that you can compare it to the `EOF` character.
3. Use the character library functions instead of writing similar ones yourself to reduce the debugging time of your program.

PROBLEMS

Data Filters. Programs called **data filters** are often used to read the information in a data file and then analyze the contents. In many cases, this data filter program is designed to remove any data errors that would cause problems with other programs that read the information from the data file. The following set of programs is designed to perform error checking and data analysis on information in a data file. Generate data files to test all features of the programs.

1.   Write a program that reads a data file that should contain only integer values, and thus should contain only digits, plus or minus signs, and white space. The program should print any invalid characters located in the file, and, at the end, it should print a count of the invalid characters located.

2.   Write a program that analyzes a data file that has been determined to contain only integer values and white space. The program should print the number of lines in the file and the number of integer values (not integer digits).

3.   Write a program that reads a file that contains only integers, but some of the integers have embedded commas, as in 145,020. The program should copy the information to a new file, removing any commas from the information. Do not change the number of values per line in the file.

Bar Graphs. Characters can be used to print a bar graph that corresponds to a set of numerical values. For example, the following bar graph corresponds to the integers 5, 9, 2, 4, 10, 7:

```
5    *****
9    *********
2    **
4    ****
10   **********
7    *******
```

4.   Write a function that receives an integer array and an integer variable that contains the number of integer values in the array. If all the values are between 0 and 50, print a bar graph similar to one shown above and return a value of 0; otherwise, do not print a bar graph, and return a value of 1. Assume that the corresponding function prototype statement is

```
int bargraph_1(int count, int data[]);
```

Cryptography. The science of developing secret codes has interested many people for centuries. Some of the simplest codes involve replacing a character or a group of characters with another character or group of characters. To easily decode these messages, the decoder needs the "key" that shows the replacement characters. In recent times, computers have been used very successfully to decode many codes that initially were assumed to be unbreakable. The next set of problems considers simple codes and schemes for decoding them. Generate files to test the programs.

6

5. A simple code can be developed by replacing each character by another character that is a fixed number of positions away in the collating sequence. For example, if each character is replaced by the character that is two characters to the right, then the letter 'a' is replaced by the letter 'c', the letter 'b' is replaced by the letter 'd', and so on. Write a program that reads the text in a file, and then generates a new file that contains the coded text using this scheme. Do not change the newline characters or the EOF character.

6. Write a program to decode the scheme presented in problem 5. Test the program using files generated by problem 5.

7. One step in decoding a simple code such as the one described in problem 5 involves counting the number of occurrences of each character. Then, knowing that the most common letter in English is 'e', the letter that occurs most commonly in the coded message is replaced by 'e'. Similar replacements are then made based on the number of occurrences of characters in the coded message and the known occurrences of characters in the English language. This decoding often provides enough of the correct replacements that the incorrect replacements can be determined. For this problem, write a program that reads a data file and determines the number of occurrences of each of the characters in the file. Then, print the characters and the number of times that they occurred. If a character does not occur, do not print it. (HINT: Use an array to store the occurrences of the characters, based on their ASCII codes.)

8. Another simple code encodes a message in text such that the true message is represented by the first letter of each word. There are not spaces between the decoded words, but the decoded string of characters can easily be separated into words by a person. Write a program to read a data file and determine the secret message stored by the sequence of first letters of the words.

9. Write a program that encodes the text in a data file using an integer array named **key** that contains 26 characters. This key is read from the keyboard. The first letter contains the character that is to replace the letter **a** in the data file, the second letter contains the letter that is to replace the letter **b** in the data file, and so on. Assume that all punctuation is to be replaced by spaces. Check to be sure that the key does not map two different characters to the same one during the encoding.

10. Write a program that decodes the file that is the output of problem 9. Assume that the same integer **key** is read from the keyboard by this file, and is used in the decoding steps. Note that you will not be able to restore the punctuation characters.

Appendix A
ASCII Character Codes

The following table contains the 128 ASCII characters and their equivalent integer values and binary values. The characters that correspond to the integers 1 through 31 have special significance to the computer system. For example, the character BEL is represented by the integer 7 and causes the bell to sound on the keyboard.

The order of the characters from low to high represents the collating sequence; it has several interesting characteristics. Note that the digits are less than uppercase letters, and uppercase letters are less than lowercase letters. Also, note that special characters are not grouped together—some are before digits, some are after digits, and some are between uppercase and lowercase characters.

Character	Integer Equivalent	Binary Equivalent
NUL (Blank)	000	0000000
SOH (Start of Header)	001	0000001
STX (Start of Text)	002	0000010
ETX (End of Text)	003	0000011
EOT (End of Transmission)	004	0000100
ENQ (Enquiry)	005	0000101
ACK (Acknowledge)	006	0000110
BEL (Bell)	007	0000111
BS (Backspace)	008	0001000
HT (Horizontal Tab)	009	0001001
LF (Line Feed or Newline)	010	0001010
VT (Vertical Tabulation)	011	0001011
FF (Form Feed)	012	0001100
CR (Carriage Return)	013	0001101
SO (Shift Out)	014	0001110
SI (Shift In)	015	0001111
DLE (Data Link Escape)	016	0010000
DC1 (Device Control 1)	017	0010001
DC2 (Device Control 2)	018	0010010

DC3 (Device Control 3)	019	0010011
DC4 (Device Control 4-Stop)	020	0010100
NAK (Negative Acknowledge)	021	0010101
SYN (Synchronization)	022	0010110
ETB (End of Text Block)	023	0010111
CAN (Cancel)	024	0011000
EM (End of Medium)	025	0011001
SUB (Substitute)	026	0011010
ESC (Escape)	027	0011011
FS (File Separator)	028	0011100
GS (Group Separator)	029	0011101
RS (Record Separator)	030	0011110
US (Unit Separator)	031	0011111
SP (Space)	032	0100000
!	033	0100001
"	034	0100010
#	035	0100011
$	036	0100100
%	037	0100101
&	038	0100110
' (Closing Single Quote)	039	0100111
(	040	0101000
)	041	0101001
*	042	0101010
+	043	0101011
, (Comma)	044	0101100
- (Hyphen)	045	0101101
. (Period)	046	0101110
/	047	0101111
0	048	0110000
1	049	0110001
2	050	0110010
3	051	0110011
4	052	0110100
5	053	0110101
6	054	0110110
7	055	0110111
8	056	0111000
9	057	0111001
:	058	0111010
;	059	0111011
<	060	0111100
=	061	0111101
>	062	0111110
?	063	0111111
@	064	1000000
A	065	1000001

B		066	1000010
C		067	1000011
D		068	1000100
E		069	1000101
F		070	1000110
G		071	1000111
H		072	1001000
I		073	1001001
J		074	1001010
K		075	1001011
L		076	1001100
M		077	1001101
N		078	1001110
O		079	1001111
P		080	1010000
Q		081	1010001
R		082	1010010
S		083	1010011
T		084	1010100
U		085	1010101
V		086	1010110
W		087	1010111
X		088	1011000
Y		089	1011001
Z		090	1011010
[		091	1011011
\		092	1011100
]		093	1011101
^	(Circumflex)	094	1011110
_	(Underscore)	095	1011111
'	(Opening Single Quote)	096	1100000
a		097	1100001
b		098	1100010
c		099	1100011
d		100	1100100
e		101	1100101
f		102	1100110
g		103	1100111
h		104	1101000
i		105	1101001
j		106	1101010
k		107	1101011
l		108	1101100
m		109	1101101
n		110	1101110
o		111	1101111
p		112	1110000

q	113	1110001
r	114	1110010
s	115	1110011
t	116	1110100
u	117	1110101
v	118	1110110
w	119	1110111
x	120	1111000
y	121	1111001
z	122	1111010
{	123	1111011
|	124	1111100
}	125	1111101
~	126	1111110
DEL (Delete/Rubout)	127	1111111

Complete Solutions to Practice! Problems

SECTION 2.2, PAGE 26

1. valid
2. valid
3. invalid character (-), replacement `tax_rate`
4. valid
5. invalid character (^), replacement `sec_sqrd`
6. valid
7. valid
8. invalid, keyword, replacement `void_term`
9. invalid characters ((,)), replacement `fx`
10. invalid character (/), replacement `m_per_s`
11. valid
12. invalid character (.), replacement `w1_1`

SECTION 2.2, PAGE 27

1. 3.5004×10^{1} 4 digits of precision
2. 4.2×10^{-4} 1 digit of precision
3. -9.99×10^{-2} 2 digits of precision
4. $1.00000028 \times 10^{-7}$ 8 digits of precision
5. 0.0000103
6. -105000
7. -3552000
8. 0.000667

SECTION 2.2, PAGE 30

1. `#define LIGHT_SPEED 2.99792e08`
2. `#define CHARGE_E 1.602177e-19`
3. `#define G_MSS 9.8`
4. `#define G_FTSS 32`
5. `#define MOON_RADIUS 1.74e06`

SECTION 2.3, PAGE 34

1. **6**   2. **4.5**   3. **3**   4. **3.0**

SECTION 2.3, PAGE 36

1. `tension = (2*m1*m2*g)/(m1 + m2);`
2. `P2 = P1 + rho*V2*V2*(A2*A2 - A1*A1)/(2*A1*A1);`

3. $\text{centripetal} = \dfrac{4\pi^2 r}{T^2}$

4. $\text{change} = GM_E m \left(\dfrac{1}{R_E} - \dfrac{1}{R_E + h} \right)$

SECTION 2.3, PAGE 39

1. x `3`   y `4`   z `8`
2. x `3`   y `4`   z `12`
3. x `6`   y `4`
4. x `2`   y `0`

SECTION 2.4, PAGE 43

1. `Sum =  150`
   `Average =  12.3680`
2. `Sum and Average`

   `150 12.4`
3. `   12.37 is the average;`
   `      150 is the sum`

4.   **12.37 is the average;   150 is the sum**

SECTION 2.5, PAGE 47

1.   **-3**   2.   **-2**   3.   **0.125**   4.   **3.16**

SECTION 2.5, PAGE 48

1.   **length = k*sqrt(1 - (v/c)*(v/c));**

2.   **center = 38.1972*(r*r*r - s*s*s)*sin(a)/((r*r - s*s)*a);**

3. $\text{range} = \dfrac{v_0{}^2}{g}\sin 2\theta$

4. $v\ \mathbf{D}\ \mathbf{s}\ \dfrac{2gh}{1\ \mathbf{C}\ \frac{\text{I}}{mr^2}}$

SECTION 3.2, PAGE 67

1.   true   2.   true   3.   true   4.   true
5.   true   6.   false

SECTION 3.3, PAGE 72

1.    ```
if (time > 15)
    time += 1;
```

2.    ```
if (sqrt(poly) < 0.5)
    printf("poly = %f \n",poly);
```

3.    ```
if (abs(volt_1-volt_2) > 10)
    printf("volt_1: %f, volt_2: %f \n",volt_1,volt_2);
```

4.    ```
if (log(x) >= 3)
{
    time = 0;
    count--;
}
```

5.    ```
if (dist<50.0 && time>10)
    time += 2;
else
    time += 2.5;
```
```

```
6.  if (dist >= 100)
        time += 2;
    else
         if (50<dist && dist<100)
        time += 1;
    else
        time += 0.5;
```

SECTION 3.4, PAGE 77

1.	18	2.	18	3.	17
4.	9	5.	infinite loop	6.	11

SECTION 4.2, PAGE 111

1.

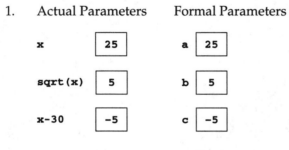

2. 2

SECTION 5.1, PAGE 122

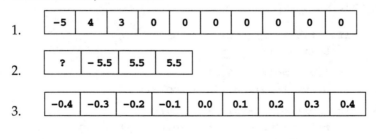

SECTION 5.1, PAGE 125

1. 3 8   2.   8 30
    15 21
    30 41

SECTION 5.1, PAGE 127

1. **9.8**   2. **9.8**   3. **3.2**   4. **1.5**

SECTION 6.1, PAGE 137

1. 40
2. 60
3. 71
4. 103
5. O
6. $
7. u
8. ^

Index

OPERATOR PRECEDENCE

Precedence	Operation	Associativity	Page
1	( ) [ ]	innermost first	34, 46, 120
2	+ - ++ -- (type) !	right to left (unary)	24, 33, 37, 66
3	* / %	left to right	32
4	+ -	left to right	32
5	< <= > >=	left to right	65
6	== !=	left to right	65
7	&&	left to right	66
8	||	left to right	66
9	= += -= *= /= %=	right to left	30, 38

COMMON C FUNCTIONS

Elementary Math Functions

ceil(x)	exp(x)	fabs(x)	floor(x)
log(x)	log10(x)	pow(x,y)	sqrt(x)

Trigonometric Functions

acos(x)	asin(x)	atan(x)	atan2(y,x)
cos(x)	sin(x)	tan(x)	

Character Functions

isalnum(c)	isalpha(c)	iscntrl(c)	isdigit(c)
isgraph(c)	islower(c)	isprint(c)	ispunct(c)
isspace(c)	isupper(c)	isxdigit(c)	tolower(c)
toupper(c)			

COMMON NUMERIC CONVERSION SPECIFIERS

Variable Type	Output Specifier	Input Specifier
int	%i, %d	%i, %d
float	%f, %e, %E, %g, %G	%f, %e, %E, %g, %G
double	%f, %e, %E, %g, %G	%lf, %le, %lE, %lg, %lG3

C STATEMENT SUMMARY

Preprocessor directives

```
#include <stdio.h>
#define PI 3.141593
```

Declarations

```
int year_1, year_2, count=0, n[]={2,4,6};
double x[25];
char c= '*';
FILE *sensor1;
double sinc(double x);
```

Assignment statement

```
area = 0.5*base*(height_1 + height_2);
```

I/O statement

```
printf("The area is %f square feet \n", area);
scanf("%i", &year);
fscanf(sensor1, "%lf %lf", &t, &motion);
fprintf(balloon, "%f %f %f\n", time, altitude, velocity);
c = getchar();
putchar(c);
```

Program exit statements

```
return EXIT_SUCCESS;
return count;
return;
```

If statements

```
if (d <= 30)
   velocity = 4.25 + 0.00175*d*d;
else
   velocity = 0.65 + 0.12*d - 0.0025*d*d;
```

While loop

```
while (degrees <= 360)
{
   printf("%6.0f %9.6f \n", degrees, degrees*PI/180);
   degrees += 10;
}
```

Do/while loop

```
do
{
   printf("%6.0f %9.6f \n", degrees, degrees*PI/180);
   degrees += 10;
} while (degrees <= 360);
```

For loop

```
for (degrees=0; degrees<=360; degrees+=10)
   printf("%6.0f %9.6f \n",degrees, degrees*PI/180);
```

File open/close functions

```
sensor1 = fopen("sensor1.dat","r");
fclose(sensor1);
```